A PERFECT SEASON

COACH PHILLIP FULMER

WITH JEFF HAGOOD

FOREWORD BY JOHN WARD

Rutledge Hill Press®
Nashville, Tennessee

Copyright © 1999 by Phillip Fulmer

All rights reserved. Written permission must be secured from the publisher to use or reproduce any part of this book, except for brief quotations in critical reviews or articles.

Tom Raymond photos, cover photo, and back-cover photos were made available through the University of Tennessee Sports Information Department.

Tim Clark, Courtland Richards, and Steve Woltmann photos reprinted by permission of Athlon Sports.

Published in Nashville, Tennessee, by Rutledge Hill Press® Inc., 211 Seventh Avenue North, Nashville, TN 37219.

Design by Harriette Bateman

Typography by Roger A. DeLiso, Rutledge Hill Press®

Digital prepress by Commercial Engraving, Nashville

Library of Congress Cataloging-in-Publication Data
Fulmer, Phillip.
    A perfect season / Phillip Fulmer with Jeff Hagood : foreword by John Ward.
      p. cm.
    ISBN 1-55853-798-8
    1. University of Tennessee, Knoxville—Football—History.   2. Tennessee Volunteers (Football team)—History.   I. Hagood, Jeff, 1960– . II. Title.
GV958.U586F86   1999
796.332'63'0976885—dc21   99-38547
                                                            CIP

2 3 4 5 6 7 8 9—04 03 02 01 00 99

CONTENTS

Foreword 4
Preface 5
Introduction 7

1. Laying the Foundation 13
2. Winter, Spring, and Summer 19
3. Fall Practice 41
4. Syracuse 45
5. Florida 53
6. Houston 63
7. Auburn 71
8. Georgia 79
9. Alabama 87
10. South Carolina 99
11. Alabama-Birmingham 107
12. Arkansas 113
13. Kentucky 123
14. Vanderbilt 129
15. Mississippi State: The SEC Championship Game 135
16. Florida State: The Fiesta Bowl 143

FOREWORD

Every Tennessee football fan has a special memory of the 1998 National Championship season.

In this book, Coach Phillip Fulmer shares his own special memories of the 13-0 season, culminating in the Fiesta Bowl victory for the national title.

Coach Fulmer gives you insight into how decisions were made on the sidelines…how preparations differed from opponent to opponent on the practice field…how coaches and players adapted to injury or the unexpected.

As you enjoy this behind-the-scenes story of Coach Fulmer's memories, here's an idea: Feel free to pencil in your own special memories of each game in the margin of the page. By the time you're finished, both you and the head coach will have written the story of the season. Coach Fulmer won't mind at all.

Thanks to all of you for being a part of Tennessee's National Championship.

John Ward
Vol Radio Network

PREFACE

A season like 1998 doesn't just happen, and there is no one reason or one person that makes it happen. So many people had their hands on this success, as is the case with any championship—family, players, coaches, Dr. Joe Johnson, John Ward, and support groups.

I want to thank my wife, Vicky, and my children for letting me do my job, for encouraging and supporting me, and for loving me. They are truly my greatest blessing from God. I thank the players on this team as well as all the men who ever put the orange and white on—they all had a piece of this building onto our tradition. Thanks, too, to the coaches who worked so hard and long to make this year happen and who were professional in the way they handled themselves.

I especially want to say thank-you to Dr. Johnson and his wife, Pat. Dr. Joe gave me a chance, and he has been extremely supportive of our efforts and a guiding light for me personally and professionally. It was special in itself that we could win a national championship in the year that he retired. I certainly wish him a long, healthy, and happy retirement. He deserves it. For thirty-eight years, Dr. Joe has touched the University of Tennessee with a loving hand.

It took me a couple of years to get things going around me like I wanted, and athletic director Doug Dickey has been there every step. I thank him for giving me a chance, for his support and guidance, and for his friendship. He is still my coach, and I admire and respect him very much. He has been and will continue to be an incredible influence in my life.

I was also pleased we could win a championship the same year John Ward and Bill Anderson retired. They have been the voices that have brought the excitement to the people for thirty-one years. John is a dear friend.

When I said it took me a couple of years to get things like I wanted, I was referring to our support groups. It takes so many people to make a program at the level of ours to work as it should. The support groups are the key to the success of our organization. The Student Life office, headed by Carmen Tegano and assisted by Judy Jackson, Lois Prislovsky, and Tyler Johnson, has been excellent when it comes to advising and supporting our players academically.

Mike Rollo and his staff in the training room have done a great job. I said more than once that if we had an MVP for the 1998 season, it was Mike Rollo. He and Dr. Val Gene Iven and his assistants, especially Keith Clements, deserve a lion's share of credit for their efforts in getting Shaun Ellis, Ron Green, and Billy Ratliff ready to play in '98 when percentages would tell you that shouldn't have happened.

John Stucky and his staff have done an incredible job in the strength and conditioning area. We do not go on the field overmatched physically if a youngster has been in the program long enough for John to do his magic. John is also an incredible influence from a spiritual standpoint, and is one of the finest Christian men I know.

I tell everyone that I want to coach and recruit and not get bogged down in paperwork and administrative duties. I thank Gary Wyant, an outstanding football operations director who was replaced by Condredge Holloway, who in turn has done a good job as well. A special thanks to David Blackburn and Scott Altizer who administered the recruiting organization.

I also say a special thank-you to Pat Pryor, my secretary who does a wonderful job keeping me on track and on time. Thanks to all of our secretaries; they all do a great job for us.

Joe Harrington and his group in the videotape department do a wonderful job giving us a competitive edge and adding a lot of personality to our world of video, computers, and film study.

Most of all, I say thank-you to my close friends—you know who you are. You are always there—in good times or tough times. A man is lucky to have a few good friends. I've been very blessed with mine.

INTRODUCTION

The final seconds were ticking off the clock. I knew the scene around me would soon be chaotic as players from both teams converged around the middle of the field, so I decided to leave the sidelines with a few seconds left on the clock. As I jogged toward midfield, things were almost a blur. There was an army of photographers, players, and fans accumulating on the field. I will never forget the flashing of lightbulbs, as what seemed like a thousand pictures were being taken. My eyes were almost blinded by the lights. All of the cameras were pointed toward Nebraska coach Tom Osborne, as he had just won his final college game and a share of the national championship.

About an hour and a half later, stepping onto the team bus and taking my customary seat on the first row to leave the Orange Bowl, the reality of what had happened began to sink in. Our team had just been soundly beaten by an outstanding Nebraska club, the best football team in the nation. I was physically and emotionally drained, yet my mind was racing a thousand miles an hour.

My thoughts drifted to the locker room that I had just left. Our players were really hurting. I had just witnessed Peyton Manning, Leonard Little, Terry Fair, Marcus Nash, Jonathan Brown, Trey Teague, Tori Noel, and many others removing their orange jerseys for the last time. I love those guys. Many of them had been three- or four-year starters. They had been responsible for winning so many football games for the University of Tennessee. They had just won the Southeastern Conference championship, and in each of the last three seasons they had finished among the top ten teams in the country.

I had just seen for the last time the horde of reporters in the locker room huddled around Peyton Manning. Peyton had played with a lot of pain in the Orange Bowl because of an injury he had suffered in our SEC Championship victory over Auburn, and his mobility was limited throughout the game against Nebraska. But Peyton Manning, more than anything else, is a competitor. I witnessed the pain of losing on his face as he answered questions with his usual grace.

On the other side of that locker room was something that caught my eye. Several reporters were gathered around our young sophomore quarterback, Tee Martin, who had impressively led our team to a late touchdown. I can't begin to tell you the range of emotions that passed through my mind as I watched those two quarterbacks respond to the media. I had just witnessed the past and the future.

As you might expect, the bus ride back to the hotel in Miami was quiet. The quietness of the hour made my mind race even faster, if that was possible. I tried to think mostly of our seniors—not just the guys who were the stars but all of our players who just minutes ago had taken off their Tennessee uniforms for the last time. I also thought about our walk-ons, student managers, and trainers, many of whom had just had their last official experience with Tennessee football. And I thought about our coaches and all of our families who have dedicated their hearts and souls to this program.

As the bus moved through the traffic, I tried my best to follow my own rule of not making a hasty judgment about effort, execution, or preparation until I had a chance to reflect and watch the game film. Hard as I tried not to, this was one of those games that I constantly replayed quickly in my mind. I'll talk later about that. By the way, I know that all of our fans, and fans everywhere, believe it's the biggest cop-out in the world for a coach to refrain from comment on a particular play or subject until "he reviews the film." But to be honest, not all of my initial reactions are right. It's usually not fair to our players or coaches, or fans for that matter, to speculate on something when I can know the answer for sure the next day.

The bus ride back seemed like three hours, not thirty minutes. On that ride, I thought a lot about our players and staff and families, and I reflected upon the game itself. But I never really thought about the tremendous loss in personnel that we had just suffered. I guess if I had, I probably would have jumped off the bus. Seriously, I am optimistic by nature. I didn't worry about Peyton Manning and Marcus Nash losing their eligibility. I *did* worry about how the players felt after a loss. I worried about how I felt and how my coaches felt.

Finally, the bus arrived back at the hotel and one thing kept popping back in my mind the rest of the night: those reporters talking to Tee Martin. I was already thinking about next year.

Being the head football coach of the University of Tennessee is an unbelievably exciting job, but it's also very hectic. We were no sooner arriving back in Knoxville than I was preparing to leave to go to the East-West Shrine Bowl game in Palo Alto, California. I was honored to have been named the head coach of the East team in this very prestigious game.

As I was getting ready to go to California, I was really dreading it. I wasn't dreading the game, because it's a wonderful affair that raises a lot of money for Shriner hospitals. I just hated leaving, period, because it meant I would be so far away from my work at Tennessee. I felt as if I had unfinished business there, and I didn't like the bitter taste in my mouth after the Orange Bowl game. I wanted to get started on fixing what we needed to fix.

The Good Lord surely works in mysterious ways. As much as I dreaded going, being so far away allowed me the opportunity to dispassionately review what we had been doing and why we had been doing it, and what we needed to do in order to win a national-championship game. I'm not saying that I wouldn't have thought about the same sort of things and reached the same conclusions if I had been in Knoxville. I just believe it was a real blessing to have nearly a week without phone calls, appearances, administrative responsibilities, and all the other things that go with being the head football coach at the University of Tennessee. I can promise you that that week at the Shrine Bowl was a week of soul-searching, which I believe set in motion the direction of our 1998 football team.

During the flight to California, and later in my hotel room in Palo Alto, I tried not to just focus on the Orange Bowl but on our entire 1997 season. I certainly don't want to sound like I was disappointed with our 1997 team or to diminish its achievements. After all, we had won the Southeastern Conference and eleven ball games. We won the SEC Championship Game in which we had to overcome what seemed like a million turnovers. I am very proud of the 1997 team and their accomplishments, and I truly believe they helped set the groundwork for our 1998 team. But when I accepted the head-coaching job at my alma mater in November 1992, I said my goal was to take our program to another level. We all know what that meant.

INTRODUCTION 9

Reflecting back on the 1997 season and trying to figure out how to get better was a marathon, not a sprint. I felt that I couldn't just look back at the two losses, Florida and Nebraska. I also needed to look at what teams were doing that allowed them to have some success against us, even when we had won. I needed to look at us and figure out how we could distance ourselves farther from the teams that we were now beating.

My analysis after the marathon was the same as my initial reaction on the bus ride after the Orange Bowl—*we needed to be a more physical team.* We also needed to do three more things: 1) improve our turnover ratio; 2) build more depth on the defensive line; and 3) remain balanced but committed to running the ball and stopping the run. I know that recipe sounds simple, but finding and providing the necessary ingredients to make the mix perfect is tough. Spring practice is a perfect time to try to create a perfect mix.

Monthly Calendar			January 1 - 31, 1998			Fulmer
Sunday	Monday	Tuesday	Wednesday	Thursday	Friday	Saturday
28	29	30	31	1 Orange Bowl Nebraska	2	3 Left Miami for Recruiting
4 FYI AFCA Convention - Dallas Ch. 7 & Vicky Left for	5	6 4-7 - Did not attend	7 East-West Game - Palo Alto, CA	8	9	10 E-W Game 4:00 (E.T.) E.S.P.N. Stanford Stadium
11 10:00 PM Team Meet.	12 Registration (Vol Calls)	13	14 Classes Begin	15	16 2:00 - Team meeting 4:00 - Sports Performance OFFICIAL VISIT WEEKEND 16-17-18 DINNER @	17 DINNER @
18 OFFICIAL VISIT Weekend	19 (UT Holiday M.L.King)	20 Wt. Training Begins (7:30 - Team Meeting ALL SPORTS)	21	22	23 OFFICE APPOINTMENTS IN A.M. OFFICIAL VISIT WEEKEND 23-24-25 DINNER @	24 DINNER - SKY BOX
25 Courtney's 15th B'day Super Bowl San Diego	26 Begin Class Checks	27	28	29 Lv. for Charlotte Distinguished Citizen Dinner - Peyton M.	30 Recruiting	31 Weekend

INTRODUCTION 11

CHAPTER • 1

Laying the Foundation

A championship team is not developed just from winter workouts, spring practice, or two-a-days: It is a process that takes years. The right mix includes quality recruiting, sound coaching, and good character in the young men that you bring into your program. One of my favorite sayings is "We need character, not characters." I certainly did not know what to expect from our 1998 team at this point, but I knew we had talent, character, and sound coaching.

David Cutcliffe, whom we call "Cut," was our assistant head coach and offensive coordinator. His offensive staff included Randy Sanders, our running backs coach; Mark Bradley, our tight ends coach; Mike Barry, our offensive line coach; and Pat Washington, our wide receivers coach. Our defensive coordinator was John Chavis, or "Chief." On the defensive staff were Dan Brooks, defensive tackles coach; Steve Caldwell, defensive ends coach; and Kevin Ramsey, defensive backs coach.

As college football coaching staffs go, ours had a lot of continuity. I cannot tell you how important this is. This is something that I am especially proud of, because I worked hard to try to put together what was one of the best staffs in the nation. When I took this job, I immediately knew that I wanted David Cutcliffe to be my offensive coordinator. David is loyal and smart, and he is one of the hardest-working men I have ever met. Coach Cutcliffe had a very unique way of really getting close to his quarterbacks, and he managed his offensive staff extremely well. He had assisted me with the offensive line, had coached the running backs, and had coached the tight ends. He knew our offense.

While Cut was the natural choice for the offensive coordinator's job, many were skeptical of my decision to elevate John Chavis to defensive coordinator. In fact, I received a lot of criticism. What the fans did not know that I knew was that John had one of the best defensive minds that you will ever find—plus he was a Tennessee graduate. He had worked hard as linebackers coach, and he deserved the promotion. Chief grew up tough: He walked on to play at Tennessee, and he coaches like he played—full bore all the time. Our defensive staff was sound in philosophy and has been well prepared under John's watch.

Recruiting is king. A lot of head coaches generally dislike the recruiting process. Not me. I truly enjoy the challenges of recruiting. I can't overestimate the importance of it. The idea is to get good players and then coach them as hard as you can. As I looked at our upcoming team, I saw the fruits of a lot of labor in the recruiting fields. As I thought about what our offense would look like, I was excited about the prospect of quarterback Tee Martin.

Tee was a huge recruit for us, not only for the position that he played and the place where he came from, but also considering what we had to overcome to get him. Tee Martin came out of high school the same year as Tim Couch, another highly acclaimed quarterback. It's no secret that we really recruited Tim hard, and, frankly, I believed that we were going to sign him. When he committed to Kentucky, we really had to hustle to make up ground to try to get our other highest-rated player—Tee Martin. Tee was from Mobile, Alabama, an area that sends a lot of players to Auburn. Auburn, Notre Dame, and many other schools were recruiting Tee and telling him that we were only recruiting him now because Tim Couch was going someplace else. That wasn't true, but yet that was a difficult obstacle to overcome. With outstanding help from David Cutcliffe and others on our staff, we were able to sign Tee. Can you imagine what 1998 would have been like without Tee Martin?

Successful recruiting is not always about getting the most-hyped player. Take wide receiver Peerless Price for instance, Peerless is from Dayton, Ohio, and he was not that heavily recruited. Kippy Brown, our former receivers coach and currently the offensive coordinator of the Miami Dolphins, loved Peerless and thought he was a playmaker who was being overlooked. In fact, Kippy thought Peerless had as much, or more, potential as the highest-rated receivers in the recruiting services. The same was true with running back Shawn Bryson, who truly could have been our offensive MVP in 1998.

Then there was guard Spencer Riley, who had always wanted to be a Volunteer. The list goes on and on. I can't recall any players from that national class of wide receivers who have been as productive in their career as Peerless has been, and I sure wouldn't trade Peerless for any of them.

Recruiting is not just selling, it is also evaluating. Our best offensive player and one of the best football players in the nation is Jamal Lewis from Atlanta. Jamal was very highly recruited, but some teams were recruiting him as a fullback. If you watched much of Jamal on film, you knew he was the real deal at tailback. We were fortunate to beat out Nebraska for Jamal, who had a major impact on our 1997 team as a true freshman.

Look at the guys who comprised our offensive line. Jarvis Reado came from New Orleans as one of the most highly recruited players in the country, and he ended up choosing us over Florida. Chad Clifton, our other tackle, was another highly recruited young man, and we were fortunate enough to beat out Alabama and Notre Dame to get him. Cosey Coleman, from Atlanta, who has a chance to be better than anyone we have ever had, was a major recruit. North Carolina, Florida, and Georgia all fought us to sign Cosey. Mercedes Hamilton and Spencer Riley were both players who received a lot of attention during recruitment.

Can you believe defensively, how big a difference it made to our team to have Al Wilson on the field? A ton. Al is from Jackson, and we recruited him hard and were fortunate to sign him. Nebraska, Notre Dame, and everyone else in the country tried to recruit Al. Raynoch Thompson, a linebacker from New Orleans, is a tall, wiry kind of player who will knock your head off on the field if he gets the chance. He came to us a little light for a linebacker, but we thought he could grow into the position. We believed Raynoch could become an outstanding player, although not many recruiters projected him as we did. Same thing with Eric Westmoreland. The challenge for us as a staff and for these two young men was to have them gain strength and weight without losing their burst of speed.

Up front, Shaun Ellis from Anderson, South Carolina, was one of the most highly recruited players in the nation. He grew up a short distance

We were fortunate to beat out Nebraska for Jamal, who had a major impact on our 1997 team as a true freshman.

LAYING THE FOUNDATION   15

from Clemson, and most people thought he would end up there. But we recruited Shaun extremely hard, and fortunately he chose to attend the University of Tennessee. Corey Terry, another end, was an All-America junior-college player who told us early on that he would choose between us and Florida State. We were fortunate enough to sign him. Defensive tackle Billy Ratliff, one of the most enjoyable young men you could ever be around, was from Magnolia, Mississippi, where he withstood tremendous pressure from people in his community who wanted him to sign with an in-state school, but he opted to sign with the Volunteers. Darwin Walker, another big tackle, was a transfer from North Carolina State. He was heavily recruited out of high school by us, among others, but decided to go to North Carolina State, where his brother was playing. When things didn't work out there, Darwin called us and inquired about transferring. Fortunately, when Darwin had informed us initially that he was signing with N.C. State, our staff handled that news with grace and courtesy. That impressed Darwin and made him want to look us up when he decided to change schools.

In our secondary, Dwayne Goodrich and Deon Grant were two of the most heavily recruited defensive players in the nation the years they came out. Dwayne was from the Chicago area, and we had to beat Michigan and Notre Dame to land him. Deon Grant is from Augusta, Georgia, and we had to fight Florida State and Georgia to ink him. Likewise, Fred White, Andre Lott, Steve Johnson, and Gerald Griffin were all prospects coveted to the point where we had to beat out many of our conference brethren to get them to sign with us.

One final key to laying the foundation for this team was developing *character* and *leadership*. These are two words coaches use a lot. I can tell you that we probably don't use them enough. How important are they? Teams that have those two elusive qualities are successful, sometimes even perfect. Teams that don't have them rarely afford their coach the chance to write a book.

I knew we had character and leadership on this 1998 team. I knew it from their past behavior. I knew it from their zeal in the weight room in the winters. I knew it because I had gotten to know every player and nearly every family on this team from recruiting. I knew what kind of character guys we had.

Character is when you volunteer your time with the Boys and Girls Clubs like so many of our guys do. Character is when you are involved, not just in word but in deed with the Fellowship of Christian Athletes, like so many of our guys are. Character is when you visit hospitals on a regular basis: This wasn't just Jeff Hall or Shawn Bryson or Tee or the other "marquee" guys; this was an effort from just about every single guy on our team in some kind of program like that. Do we as a staff encourage it? Absolutely. But these guys have become active in groups that make a difference. That is character.

Leadership. Al Wilson has been a leader on our football team since his sophomore year. Shawn Bryson, Jeff Hall, Tee Martin, Jamal Lewis, Cedrick Wilson, Spencer Riley, Mercedes Hamilton, Billy Ratliff—these guys have been leaders in the locker room and on the practice field. Goodrich, Thompson, Westmoreland, Walker, Clifton, Coleman—these are guys who have positively influenced younger players with their work habits.

If things are close to equal, character and leadership will determine the victor. Our guys weren't perfect. They made mistakes. But I believed that if our coaches and our talent level were close to our competitors', our character and leadership on this team would give us a chance to be something special.

A big part of the leadership on our football team comes from our Unity Council. The Unity Council is elected by the team, but I have the veto power to remove anyone that doesn't live up to the standards. The purpose of the Unity Council is to be an extension of the team and a communication link from the team to our coaches. It is an honor to be a member of the Unity Council. The 1998 members were Tee Martin, Shawn Bryson, Cedrick Wilson, Peerless Price, Spencer Riley, Jarvis Reado, Ron Green, Jeff Coleman, Al Wilson, Steve Johnson, Andre Lott and Jeff Hall. Our Unity Council has a mission statement that reads:

> *[Our Mission is] To provide positive leadership for the team. To serve the team and coaches as a communication link on all issues that arise. To be proactive in facilitating the academic, social, and athletic successes of each individual on the team and most importantly to the team itself. To provide ideas, share experiences, and make suggestions for the improvement of the Volunteer Football Program.*
>
> *To express ourselves as individuals, but to serve as one voice in support of Coach Fulmer and the program in the best of times but especially in the tough times and on tough issues.*

Not only is the Unity Council a communications link from our players to our coaches, but it is also a way for me to communicate through them.

Our potential for leadership was there, but it had to be pushed to the front. We had such dominant personalities around here for so long, guys like Peyton Manning, Bill Duff, Tori Noel, and Jonathan Brown. We put off naming captains as we normally do in March. I told the seniors to show me the examples—what you do in the classroom, weight room, and community is how you show your leadership—then we'll elect our captains. This turned out to be a great decision as our team later elected outstanding captains.

CHAPTER • 2

Winter, Spring, and Summer

Between the end of the Orange Bowl and the start of spring practice, several encouraging things took place in our program. First, we had a strong year in recruiting. I felt going into recruiting that we needed to focus on signing as many quality defensive linemen as possible and as many aggressive coverage guys as we could. Also, I wanted to sign a receiver who could make a difference. I saw those as the three biggest needs of our football team. I thought we really improved ourselves where we needed help.

Second, our winter workouts were exceptional. Winter and summer are the times of the year that your team can really improve in the areas of strength, explosion, and speed. John Stucky, his staff, and I had challenged all the players on our team to make the commitment and sacrifice to improve themselves physically for the sake of the team. If our goal was to be more physical, this was where it started. Our players challenged each other. Jamal Lewis and Al Wilson, who were roommates, got into a friendly but very heated contest over who could do the most repetition of weights one day. I could see leadership starting to emerge. I was excited about this.

During this time, I hired a new coach, Mike Barry, to round out our staff. Mike was an experienced and extremely knowledgeable offensive line coach, but most importantly he had coached the offensive line for a Colorado team that had won the national championship. I felt that Mike's coaching philosophy would give us a boost in helping to develop a more physical nature to our football team.

Our staff spent the next several weeks preparing not only for spring practice but also the season ahead. Late February and early March is usually a time to catch your breath a little as a team and staff. This year was a little different for us. I believe our coaches, just like our players, were motivated by the fact that a lot of folks were saying our football team would not be nearly as good this coming year as it had been the last three or four years. We all heard the "talk on the street," that all our star players had graduated and we were headed for a major rebuilding year. Our coaches responded with outstanding effort and commitment during this key period of preparation.

These winter months are the time of year when your coaches first begin to look at tape of next year's opponents and review what our team has been doing. It's a time to research and exchange new ideas and be really introspective. The communication among our different staff members during this time was really good. We all realized as a staff that being a more physical football team was priority number one. Effective communication among a staff is so important. Our guys seemed to be pulling together as a unit and were more concerned about the team than just the positions that they coach. As head coach, that is exactly what you want. I sensed that our staff and our players really accepted the challenges that were ahead of them. I felt really good about where we were headed going into spring practice.

There is no more exciting time of the year for a football coach than spring practice. It's always a great time for optimism, and it gives you a chance to look at how your players have responded after a year or two on a weight and nutrition program. Spring practice to the coaches and the players is not just the four weeks that you work out on the practice field before the Orange and White Game, it's the culmination of months-long winter workouts. Phase 1 is the off-season. Phase 2 is Spring. Phase 3 is Summer. And Phase 4 is the season.

As I said earlier, in order for us to have a chance to compete better in a national-championship-type game, we had to be a more physical football team. What does that mean? It means a whole lot more than just running the football. Being more physical means doing better not only in weight training but also in the area of proper nutrition. Before we started our winter workouts in January, I sat down with Coach Stucky, our strength and conditioning coach, and we talked about how we could improve our team physically. I wanted our players to have more explosion. That's part of being more physical. John thought that we were in most instances maximizing ourselves in weight training, but that nutritionally we could improve. So that's what we set out to do.

Being more physical is also a mind-set. At our first team meeting in January, I challenged our football players to be a more physical team. I told them the exact thing that I am telling you; for us to have a chance to win at the highest level, we had to be more physical. I told our guys that part of that was up to them, and that was my challenge to them, to compete in the weight room with a fierceness in attitude that would involve each man's pushing himself to the limit. The other part of being physical was up to their coaches, and I promised our players that they could count on us to hold up our end of the deal. I told our guys that we were getting a little bit of a reputation as being a big-play, or finesse, kind of team, and that was going to change. Our 1998 football team was going to run the football more, control the time of possession more, and we were going to be tougher on defense. We were going to run the football more in practice, and we were going to *defend* running the football more in practice. I told our guys that the green jerseys (those are the jerseys that players wear when they are to have no contact) for skill players was going to be a thing of the past and that our 1998 football team might be outsmarted or outcoached, but it was not going to be "out-toughed." That first team meeting of 1998 had an impact.

Our entire football staff felt exactly as I did before that first team meeting. We as a staff made a commitment to refocus on prioritizing the running game in our offense and being a tougher and more physical football team.

Spring practice is not only an exciting time but also a fun time for coaches. The challenge is not to get ready for next week's opponent, but to work with your guys and hopefully make them better. There is always enthusiasm and excitement with the beginning of spring work. Everybody is undefeated, and there are positions to hold onto, positions to win, and depth to build. In spring practice, we think players…not plays!

At our first team meeting of the spring, we started out with a silent prayer for Shaun Ellis, who had recently been involved in a serious car accident and was lucky to be alive. The mood was somber after that, but the players were still very attentive. I told them that our team had its own

> **I told our guys that we were getting a little bit of a reputation as being a big-play, or finesse, kind of team, and that was going to change.**

unique set of challenges as well as doubters out there. I said that the effort and commitment they made over the spring and summer would determine what their 1998 season would be like. I asked them to look around the room and see who they depended on to make their team successful—for if they were to be successful their eyes would look at every man in that room. I emphasized the need for a team effort.

I told our team that three factors would determine our success in 1998: 1) how *physical* we were; 2) an *attitude* focused on effort, enthusiasm, and commitment; and 3) having *leadership* on and off the field. I closed the meeting by asking them where they wanted to be in nine months, and I reminded them that every player and coach in the room controlled that.

We had twenty good days of spring practice. We didn't always have the best execution or the best rhythm, but we really had outstanding effort. Practices were more physical. Everybody who wasn't injured was either hitting or being hit throughout most of the spring, including Tee Martin. In past years, many of our quarterbacks and wide receivers wore green jerseys (remember, don't hit) during the spring. Like I said, we changed that this year. I figured if we were going to be a more physical football team in the fall, we had better start practicing that way in the spring.

Some players were stepping up or emerging at positions where we needed help. Deon Grant was more comfortable in our defense and was showing some of his big-play ability. Steve Johnson and Andre Lott were making progress at the corner positions. Eric Westmoreland was developing into a linebacker that you could win with in our league. Defensive tackle Darwin Walker was becoming a player the offense had to pay attention to when he was on the field. Corey Terry and DeAngelo Lloyd were improving at our defensive end positions.

Offensively, Tee Martin was taking charge in the huddle and was getting a much better command of our offense. The other offensive players were rallying around Tee—he was exhibiting good leadership. Cedrick Wilson and David Martin were encouraging in their showing of improvement at wide receiver. Shawn Bryson was emerging as a real threat at fullback. I thought he had a chance to be one of the best fullbacks in the country. Jamal Lewis was certainly going to be a major force at tailback, and Travis Henry and Travis Stephens were rapidly improving as running backs. Cosey Coleman,

Spencer Riley, Chad Clifton, and Mercedes Hamilton were developing not only into quality players, but leaders of our offensive line. This group, I thought, had a chance to be the best in our conference.

Jeff Hall and David Leaverton both kicked exceptionally well in the spring. Jeff was accurate and so dependable, while David had a monster leg and was far more consistent in the spring than he had been the previous season.

Coming out of spring practice, I had a very positive feeling about our team. I felt as if we had enough talent, and I liked our mix of returning players and emerging players. Perhaps more than anything else, I thought our football team was more physical during spring practice and that the attitude and leadership of our players was just what I wanted it to be.

After spring practice concluded, I called a team meeting for a very important purpose—to elect captains for our 1998 football team, the defending SEC Champions. I started off the meeting by addressing our veteran players and reminding them that they had been like "little brothers" around here for a long time, looking to a Peyton Manning, Leonard Little, or Marcus Nash for leadership for our team. Now, it was time for them to walk out of the shadows and step up to become the leaders of *this* team. I told our players before they voted to think about who they wanted as leaders, as examples, and as spokesmen for our football program. I told them this wasn't a popularity contest and wrote down on a board what my expectations were:

1) Elect a person you are proud to have represent you and this program.
2) Elect someone whose academics are in order.
3) Elect someone who socially has, and will be, a good representative for us.
4) Athletically elect:
   a) A team player, not a selfish guy.
   b) A dependable person.
   c) A fighter when times are tough.
   d) A guy with character who will be doing the right things when the coach is not looking.
   e) A guy who will speak up to the team.
   f) A guy who will speak for the team.

Our players took good advice. They selected Shawn Bryson, Al Wilson, Jeff Hall, and Mercedes Hamilton as captains.

At the conclusion of spring workouts, our coaches have about a month in which they can visit high schools and evaluate potential recruits. Following that, we have our football camp the first couple of weeks in June, which keeps our coaches very busy. The rest of June is spent looking at our opponents and beginning some preliminary preparation for our games. I try to give our staff about three weeks off during July to let them spend much-needed time with their families and hopefully allow them to recharge their batteries. Our coaches invest a tremendous amount of time and effort toward our program, and so far in 1998 they had hit it harder than ever.

Most of our players stayed in Knoxville, attended summer school, and worked out on their own. I told our guys at the end of spring practice that the most important time of the year for each of them was the summer. That time determines whether they will work to improve themselves physically and be in top shape for fall practice, or whether they will loaf all summer and try to get in shape during fall practice.

The summer of 1998 had more of our players in the weight room, out running sprints, and hanging around each other and around our football complex than at any other time in my tenure. It just wasn't me. Our whole staff noticed this increased effort. You could tell there was something special about this group.

Our doctors and Mike Rollo and his staff did a great job over the summer in working with our injured players like Shaun Ellis, Billy Ratliff, and Ron Green in getting them ready to play.

As the summer rolled toward its end, the enthusiasm around our place was high and the excitement was starting to build. Fall practice was just ahead. Syracuse was just ahead. I couldn't wait.

OFFENSIVE PRACTICE SCHEDULE

WORKOUT: #1
GEAR: SHORTS
PLACE: HUDSON

DATE: TUESDAY, MARCH 17, 1998
TIME: 2:00 Meetings, 3:00 Flex
WINNING EDGE: EFFORT

Spring Football Schedules (text resumes on page 41)

	C-G	T	TE's	WR	QB	RB
● PER ME						
1 3:10	S-S PULLS L/R PASS WAVE L/R	<----------	S-S FINISH DRILL CHUTES&BOARD	PUNT W/QB's	BAGS DROPS WARM UP AGILITIES	PUNT
2 3:20	FIT DRILL CHUTES-BASE-FINISH	WINNING EDGE REACH BLOCK	BLOCKING 2 MAN SLED DON'T LOOK BACK	CIRCUIT	BALL SEC. BALL HANDLING BAGS	2ndEFFORT
3 3:30	BASE LB's DOWN SETS	- - - - - - -	REACH BLOCK 7 TECH WORK CONE DRILLS		S/S	<---------- T/A
4 3:40	ZONE L/R ONSIDE BACKSIDE	<----------------	BLOCKING CORNER UP & CORNER BACK	DALLAS	DRILL	RVA ---------->
5 3:50	POP&TURN L/R COMBOS EVEN SCHEME BACK CALL	<------------	<---------- RVA		VOL ROLL STRIP DR BALL SEC
6 4:00 ●	MIDDLE DRILL	<-----------------------	<---------- RVA		MIDDLE DRILL
7 4:10	MIDDLE DRILL	<-----------------------	<---------- 1 ON 1 ---------->		MIDDLE DRILL
8 4:20	PASS SET's KICK/POWER PUNCH DRILL	<----------	OUTSIDE ------------>		
9 4:30	B.P.U. 60-80	- - - - - - -	OUTSIDE ------------>		
10 4:40	TEAM - SPLIT - RUN 1's - 2's ------------>					
11 4:50	TEAM - SPLIT - RUN - PLAY ACTION - 80's ------------>		1's	2's		
12 5:00	TEAM - PASS VS DEFENSE ------------>					
13 5:10 ●	CIRCUIT		Randy-Bags Mike-4 way wave drill Mark-4pt seat roll			
14			Pat-Lateral Wave PERFECT PLAYS			

OFFENSIVE PRACTICE SCHEDULE

WORKOUT: #2
GEAR: SHORTS
PLACE: STADIUM

DATE: WEDNESDAY, MARCH 18, 1998
TIME: 3:45 FLEX
WINNING EDGE: BALL SECURITY

PER	C-G	T	TE's	WR	QB	RB
1 4:00	X PT & FG - X PT & FG	<--------------------->	S/S CONES	BAGS/AGIL. DROPS WARM UP	WARM UP THROWING	WARM UP BAGS BALL SEC
2 4:10	DIG OUTS	<----------- WINNING EDGE ------>	GL DIG OUTS	BALL DRILL	CIRCUIT - BLOCKING	THROWING ON RUN	BALL DRILLS
3 4:20	ETHYL/EVEN	<-----------	U JET FISH HOOKS	BALL SEC. PUSH/CRACK VS COVER 8	T/A	<---------
4 4:30	POP & TURN	<-----------	Head Up vs Motion Man/Zone 2's v/Ballas Ball Drills	DALLAS	DRILL
5 4:40	BPU - NAKED <------------------- 60/80/880	RVA ----------->	BPU
6 4:50	MIDDLE DRILL <-----------	RVA ----------->	MIDDLE DRILL
7 5:00	G.L. MIDDLE DRILL <-----------	1 ON 1 ----------->	G.L. MIDDLE DRILL
8 5:10	PASS SET's <------------------- 60/80/880	OUTSIDE ----------->
9 5:20	PUNCH DRILL SETS VS TWISTS	OUTSIDE ----------->
10 5:30	TEAM - G.L. VS SCOUTS ----------->
11 5:40	TEAM - SPLIT ----------->
12 5:50	TEAM - DEFENSE ----------->
13 6:00	AGILITY CIRCUIT
14						

26   A PERFECT SEASON

WINTER, SPRING, AND SUMMER   27

OFFENSIVE PRACTICE SCHEDULE

WORKOUT: #3
DATE: THURSDAY, MARCH 19, 1998
GEAR: FULL PADS   **TIME:** 2:00 MEETINGS; 3:05 FLEX & FG
PLACE: STADIUM   WINNING EDGE: PHYSICAL PLAY

Time	#	C-G	T	TE's	WR	QB	RB
	PER						
3:20	1	BASE/LB BLK <---------	PUNT	PUNT	PUNT W/QB's	BAGS/AGIL. DROPS WARM UP	PUNT
3:30	2	DIG OUTS <------------ BLOCKING -CIRCUIT- WINNING EDGE		BALL DRILLS	S & S	FOOTWORK	PASS FT WORK
3:40	3	MIDDLE DRILL <------------------		BLOCKING VS 8, VS 1, VS 2		MIDDLE DRILL <------	
3:50	4	TENNESSEE DRILL <--------------------------------					
4:00	5	SCHEME DRILL <------------------		RABBIT DRILL W/DB's	Throwing on Run Screen Throws Throwing Dr.	VS LB's PASS PRO 1 ON 1 ROUTES	
4:10	6	POP&RTURN COMBO, ZONE <------------		RVA <---------		QUICK GAME WORK	
4:20	7	9 ON 8 <-----------------------		1 ON 1 VS DB's <---------		9 ON 8	
4:30	8	PUNCH PASS SET/ <--------------	OUTSIDE <---------------	ORANGE AREA			
4:40	9	LOVERS LANE <---------------	OUTSIDE <----------------------				
4:50	10	TEAM VS SCOUTS <----------------------------------					
5:00	11	TEAM - SPLIT <----------------------------------					
5:10	12	TEAM VS DEFENSE <----------------------------------					
	13						
	14						

OFFENSIVE PRACTICE SCHEDULE

WORKOUT: #4
GEAR: FULL PADS
PLACE: U. HUDSON

DATE: TUESDAY, MARCH 31, 1998
TIME: 2:00 MEETINGS; 3:10 FLEX & FG
WINNING EDGE: FUNDAMENTALS

TIME	PER	C-G	T	TE'S	WR	QB	RB
3:25	1	BASE/COMBO	<---------	S & S G OPTION	PUNT/ W/QB's	WITH WR's	PUNT
3:35	2	<----------------- BLOCKING CIRCUIT ----------------->					
		16-17/14-15 G PULLS	TAC/DOWN	FISH HOOK	S & S	RUN GAME MECHANICS	
3:45	3	BLUNT POP - PULL	<------------	SLED BLOCK 50 PRO BALL DRILLS	BLOCKING DRILLS	T/A	<---------
3:55	4	PERIMETER	<------------	ROUTE WORK W/QB's	BALL DRILLS	<--------	PERIMETER - - -
4:05	5	MIDDLE DRILL	<-------------------------	PERIMETER & QK GAME	RVA	<--------	MIDDLE DRILL
4:15	6	MIDDLE DRILL	<-------------------------	PLAY ACTION	RVA	<------>	MIDDLE DRILL
4:25	7	9 ON 8	<-------------------------	DB PASS	RVA	<---------	9 ON 8
4:35	8	BPU VS DEFENSE	<------------	1 ON 1 VS DB's		<---------	BPU VS DEFENSE
4:45	9	LOVERS LANE	<------------	OUTSIDE (SPLIT)			
4:55	10	TEAM - SPLIT VS DEFENSE ------------------------					<--------
5:05	11	TEAM - SPLIT VS DEFENSE ------------------------					<--------
5:15	12	TEAM - PASS VS DEFENSE ------------------------					<--------
5:25	13	AGILITY	CIRCUIT -	PERFECT PLAYS			
	14						

OFFENSIVE PRACTICE SCHEDULE

WORKOUT: #5
GEAR: FULL PADS
PLACE: U. HUDSON

DATE: THURSDAY, APRIL 2, 1998
TIME: 2:00 MEETINGS; 3:10 FLEX
WINNING EDGE; INTENSITY; SENSE OF URGENCY

	C-G	T	TE'S	WR	QB	RB
1 3:20	BASE/PULLS	<---------	LB BLOCKS S & S	PUNT RETURN	BAGS AGILITIES S&S	PR/BALL DRILLS/ OK GAME
2 3:30	CAGE LEFT	GATE/P SLIP <--------- <-----WINNING EDGE----> -------BLOCKING CIRCUITS--------		S & S	OPT.FOOTWORK BAGS PITCHES RIGHT	GAUNTLET
3 3:40	CAGE LEFT CAGE RIGHT	GATE/PSLIPRT - - - - - GATE/PSLIPLT <---------	BLOCKING DRILLS	THROWING MECHANICS PERIMETER	VOL. ROLL SIDELINE MED.BALL LAUNCH
4 3:50	16/17 G OPTION PULLS RT	<--------- PULLS LEFT	BALL DRILLS	T/A <-------->	
5 4:00	MIDDLE DRILL	<------------------------	<---------- RVA ---------->	MIDDLE DRILL
6 4:10	BLITZ PICK UP	<------------------------	<---------- RVA ---------->	B.P.U.
4:20	LOVERS LANE	<-------------	<------------ OUTSIDE (SPLIT) ------------->	
8 4:30	S C R I M M A G E		6 PLAYS MAXIMUM		
9			4 W/EACH GROUP (SPLIT)		
10			8 PUNTS BETWEEN SERIES X PT PG		
11		AGILITY CIRCUITS TO FOLLOW			
12					
13					
14					

WINTER, SPRING, AND SUMMER 29

OFFENSIVE PRACTICE SCHEDULE

WORKOUT: #6
DATE: FRIDAY, APRIL 3, 1998
GEAR: FULL PADS
TIME: 4:00 DEF. DRILLS;4:30 OFF.DRILLS;4:55 FLEX;5:00
PLACE: U. HUDSON
WINNING EDGE: EFFORT;BE SET W/MOTION
PERIOD 1

PER	C-G	T	TE'S	WR	QB	RB
Drills 4:30	BASE/LB's	BASE/LB's	<----BLOCKING CIRCUIT---->	BAGS S&S	BAGS	
4:40	BASE/LB's <----------	S & S	C-B S & S	BLOCKING DRILLS	WARM UP SHIFT DR.	DROPS Vol.Roll/Strip/Sideline/Cones/Same FootHand Agil.-Pass Game
4:50	PASS SETS/ PUNCH <----------	DIG-OUTS BALL DRILLS	TAIL ENDS CONE DRILL	NAKEDS SCREEN DR. BLITZ THR.	BALL DR. CONE DR.
	FLEX					
1 5:00	DIG-OUTS <----------	VS DE's	BALL DRILL	THROW ON RUN	PR/LAUNCH DRILL
2 5:08	COMBO BLOCKS POP & TURN CAGE <----------	SCOOP SLED	RELEASE DRILLS	T/A <----------	
3 5:16	G.L. MIDDLE DRILL <----------		RVA --------->	G.L. MIDDLE DRILL	
4 5:24	<---------- TEAM - PERIMETER ---------->				
5 5:32	MIDDLE DRILL <----------		RVA --------->	MIDDLE DRILL	
6 5:40	BPU's 60's 50's <----------		80's 1 ON 1 VS DB's --------->	BPU	
7 5:48	PASS SETS/ PUNCH <----------	OUTSIDE <----------			
8 5:56	LOVERS LANE <----------	OUTSIDE <----------			
9 6:04	<---------- TEAM - PASS VS DEFENSE (PRESSURE) ---------->				
	AGILITY	CIRCUIT				

SATURDAY - April 4, 1998

Practice #7
Full Gear
Stadium

Winning Edge: Hustle On & Off the Field

Meetings
12:30 Flex
12:40 Ind. Warm Up
12:50 Team Take Off
12:55 Scrimmage

+40	1's	8 snaps
+40	2's	8 snaps
+9	1's	4 snaps
+3	1's	3 snaps

Field Goals – 4 Kicks

+9	2's	4 snaps
+3	2's	3 snaps

-40 Punt Return – 1 Reg. Each Group

-30	1's	8 snaps
-30	2's	8 snaps

-30 Punt & Coverage – 1 Reg. Each Group

-30	3's	10 snaps
-30	1's	8 snaps
-30	2's	8 snaps

Field Goal – 4 Kicks

-30	3's	8 snaps
-30	2's	8 snaps

Punt Protection vs Punt Block Cover 10

OFFENSIVE PRACTICE SCHEDULE

WORKOUT: #8
GEAR: FULL PADS
PLACE: U. HUDSON

DATE: TUESDAY, APRIL 7, 1998
TIME: 2:00 MEETING; 3:10 FLEX
WINNING EDGE: HUSTLE ON & OFF THE FIELD

PER TIME	C-G	T	TE's	WR	QB	RB
1 3:20	BASE/LB <-------------		FINISH S & S	PUNT/ PUNTRETURN	BAGS AGILITIES WARM UP	PUNT/ PUNT RETURN
2 3:32	<----------------WINNING EDGE - BLOCKING CIRCUIT----------------> "G" SCHEME <----------	6 TECH WORK	CONE DRILL	THROWING DRILLS	BAGS
3 3:40	B/K SCHEMES	<-- W/LB's -->	ZONE WORK SLED WORK BLOCKING DRILLS	BALL DRILL	T/A <----------	
4 3:50	B/K SCHEMES	CTR/6 T/G T/TE	1 ON 1 VS DB's	REC. GAUNTLET R W/DB's	SDLINE DR. VS LB's W/RB's	PASS PRO VS LB's <----------
5 4:00	MIDDLE DRILL <-------------------			RVA ----------		MIDDLE DRILL
6 4:10	MIDDLE DRILL <-------------------			RVA ----------		MIDDLE DRILL
7 4:20	B.P.U. <-------------------			1 ON 1 VS DB's <-------->		BPU
8 4:30	PASS PRO <----------		OUTSIDE	<----------		
9 4:40	LOVERS LANE <----------		OUTSIDE	<----------------------		
10 4:50	TEAM - SPLIT - 1's & 2's <-----------------------------------					
11 5:00	TEAM - BLITZ <-----------------------------------					
12 5:10	TEAM - PASS <-----------------------------------					
13 5:20	AGILITY	CIRCUIT				
14						

WINTER, SPRING, AND SUMMER 33

OFFENSIVE PRACTICE SCHEDULE

WORKOUT: #9
GEAR: FULL PADS
PLACE: U. HUDSON

DATE: WEDNESDAY, APRIL 8, 1998
TIME: 3:15 FLEX & FG
WINNING EDGE: STAND YOUR GROUND

PER	C-G	T	TE'S	WR	QB	RB
1 3:30	BASE/LB ---------->		PUNT 5' PUNT RETURN	PUNT/ PUNTRETURN	WARM UP SCREEN THROWS/S&S THROW DRILL	PUNT 5' PUNT RETURN 5'
2 3:40	<-------- "G" & COMBOS		S & S BALL DRILLS	BALL SEC. CONE DRILL BALL DRILL	T/A -------->	
3 3:50	MIDDLE DRILL <------------------			RVA <-----------		MIDDLE DRILL
4 4:00	SCHEMES VS DT & LB's <-----------		VS DE's	RVA <-----------		BALL SEC BLOCKING DRILLS
5 4:10	B.P.U. 60/660's <----------------------		VS DB's	1 ON 1 <---------		B.P.U.
6	IND PASS PRO WORK LOVERS LANE 2 GROUPS		OUTSIDE <------------------------			
4:20						
4:30	BACKED UP - 9 - 3 PLAYS - MINIMUM - 6 PLAYS MAX 2 SERIES 1's & 2's					
8	3RD DOWNS - 3-6 3-8 3-10 1's 3-5 3-7 3-9 2's					
9	OPEN FIELD - 30 1's 6 PLAYS 2's 6 PLAYS					
10				1's 6 PLAYS 2's 6 PLAYS		
11	AGILITY CIRCUITS <------------------------					
12						
13						
14						

OFFENSIVE PRACTICE SCHEDULE

WORKOUT: #10
DATE: THURSDAY, APRIL 9, 1998
GEAR: SHORTS
TIME: 2:00 MEETING; 3:10 FLEX, 5' IND, FG
PLACE: U. HUDSON
WINNING EDGE: 2 MINUTE DRILL PROCEDURE

	C-G	T	TE's	WR	QB	RB
PER						
1 3:25	BASE/LB ---------->		PUNT KOC 5'	KOC PUNT	S&S BAGS	PUNT FOOTWORK KOC
2	<-------------- WINNING EDGE -------------->					
3:35	ZONE STEPS ---------->		ZONE SWEEP	S & S	WARM UP	BAGS
3 3:45	CAGE/ ETHYL	ETHYL P.SLIP POP & TURN	FISH HOOKS	BALL DRILL BLOCKING CONE DRILL	<-------- T/A	
4 3:55	MIDDLE DRILL <--------------------------			RVA <------------		MIDDLE DRILLS
5 4:05	PASS PRO 60S CTR/G's 60'S	T's SETS WIDE E's	RVA <--------------------------			PASS PRO UNDER- STANDING
6 4:15	<--------- TEAM - BLITZ VS SCOUTS -------->					
7 4:25	RAMBO's <------------ 660's/80's/ 660's/80's/	BEAR/TIGER/WHAM FUNDAMENTALS PASS PRO	1 ON 1 VS DB's <-------			PASS PRO W/OL
8 4:35	G/BOSS <------------	OUTSIDE <---------------------				
9 4:45	SCREEN <------------ 960/961	MUSTANG,STALLION OUTSIDE <---------------------				
10 4:55	<--------- TEAM - BLITZ -------->					
11 5:05	<--------- TEAM - PASS -------->					
12 5:15	<--------- TEAM - 2 MINUTE DRILL - 1's -------->					
13 5:25	AGILITY	CIRCUITS				
14						

WINTER, SPRING, AND SUMMER

SCRIMMAGE #2
April 10, 1998

WORKOUT: #11
FULL GEAR
STADIUM

8:00 INDIVIDUAL MEETINGS
9:15 FLEX

WINNING EDGE: Finish

KOC – TAKE OFF 2 EACH GROUP

(1's) 8 SNAP MINIMUM

(2's) 8 SNAP MINIMUM

X PT & FG   3 KICKS

(1's) 8 SNAP MINIMUM

PUNT TEAM – 1 EACH GROUP

(2's) 8 SNAP MINIMUM

PUNT RETURN – 1 EACH GROUP

(3's) 8 SNAP MINIMUM

(1's) 2 MINUTE DRILL 6 SNAP MINIMUM

X PT & FG   4 KICKS

(2's) 8 PLAY MINIMUM

(1's & 2's) 3rd DOWNS - 6 SNAPS EACH

3rd – 7 3rd – 6
3rd – 9 3rd – 8
3rd – 5 3rd – 10

ORANGE AREA

+20 2 SERIES 1's & 2's 6 PLAY MINIMUM
X PT & FG   4 KICKS
3's (8 SNAPS)

OFFENSIVE PRACTICE SCHEDULE

WORKOUT: #12
GEAR: FULL PADS   DATE: TUESDAY, APRIL 14, 1998
PLACE: STADIUM   TIME: 2:00 MEETING; 3:15 FLEX & PUNT
                         WINNING EDGE: GREEN CHECK CADENCE

PER	C-G	T	TE'S	WR	QB	RB
1 3:30	BASE/LB <------------		KOR	KOR	BAGS AGILITIES	KOR
2 3:40	CAGE/SLANT	POP&TURN/ETHYL	S & S	W/QB's	W/TE's	CONES
	<------------------WINNING EDGE-BLOCKING CIRCUIT------------------>					
3 3:50	CAGE/ 6/7 SLANT	ETHYL POP & TURN/ ODD POP&TURN	ZONE FISH HOOKS RELEASE DRILLS	CONE DRILL	T/A <------------>	
4 4:00	SCHEME VS DEFENSE <------------		VS DE's	VS DB's	THROWING DRILLS BALL SEC.	ROUTE WORK
5 4:10	MIDDLE DRILL 4-3 <------------			RVA <-----------		MIDDLE DRILL
6 4:20	MIDDLE DRILL ODD <------------			RVA <-----------		MIDDLE DRILL
7 4:30	BPU <------------		BALL DRILLS	1 ON 1 VS DB's <--------->		BPU
8 4:40	PASS <------------ INDIVIDUAL			OUTSIDE - ORANGE AREA <--------->		
9 4:50	LOVERS <------------ LANE			OUTSIDE <--------->		
10 5:00	TEAM - VS SCOUTS - 3 DOWN <---------------------					
11 5:10	TEAM - SPLIT <---------------------					
12 5:20	TEAM - VS DEFENSE <---------------------					
13 5:30	AGILITY	CIRCUITS				
14						

OFFENSIVE PRACTICE SCHEDULE

WORKOUT: #13
GEAR: FULL PADS
PLACE: HUDSON
DATE: WEDNESDAY, APRIL 15, 1998
TIME: 3:15 FLEX & PG/3:30 PERIOD 1
WINNING EDGE: NO HUDDLE OFFENSE

PER	C-G	T	TE'S	WR	QB	RB
1 3:30	BASE/LB <-----------		S&S C-B FINISH	PUNT RETURN	AGILITIES WARM UP	PUNT RETURN
2 3:40	CAGE/POP & TURN	FISH HOOKS	ZONE FISHHOOK P&T VS ODD	S & S CONE DRILL	T/A <--------->	
3 3:50	MIDDLE DRILL	<----------------------		RVA <----------->		MIDDLE DRILL
4 4:00	BPU <------------------		BALL DRILLS	1 ON 1 VS DB's <--------->		BPU
5 4:10	TEAM VS SCOUTS <----------------------					
6 4:20	LOVERS LANE <--------------->		OUTSIDE <----------------			
7	BACKED UP <----------------		3 PLAYS EACH GROUP			
8 4:30	SHORT YARDAGE <-----------------		2 PLAYS EACH GROUP			
9	3RD DOWNS (3-1) <-----------------		6 PLAYS EACH GROUP			
10	2 MINUTE DRILL-ORANGE AREA <----------------		6 PLAYS W/1's	4 PLAYS W/2's		
			3 PLAYS EACH GROUP			
11	3RD DOWNS OPEN FIELD <-----------------		4 PLAYS EACH GROUP 3&8 3&10 3&7			
12			8 PLAYS EACH GROUP			
13						
14						

OFFENSIVE PRACTICE SCHEDULE

DATE: THURSDAY, APRIL 16, 1998
TIME: 2:00 MEETINGS; 3:40 FLEX
WINNING EDGE: PENALTY DISCIPLINE

WORKOUT: #14
GEAR: FULL PADS
PLACE: HUDSON

	C-G	T	TE'S	WR	QB	RB
3:50 1	BASE/LB's <-----------		S&S FINISH C-B	PUNT	AGILITIES WARM UP S & S	PUNT
4:00 2	CAGE/POP & TURN	HOOKS <--------	ZONE FISHHOOK COMBOS	PUNT RETURN	IND. DROPS DECIS. MAKE IND. TECHS	PUNT RETURN
4:10 3	PASS SETS 80/60 <------- TIM/BEAR/TIGER		LB BLOCKS 6 TECH CONE DRILL WORK	S & S	PERIMETER TECHS	BAGS BALL DRILLS
4:20 4	SCREEN REVIEW <-------- MUSTANG/STALLION/690,691		BALL DRILLS PASS PRO DR. BLOCKING	RUN/PASS SCH BALL DRILL	T/A <---------->	
4:30 5	MIDDLE DRILL	<--------------------	RVA	<-----------		MIDDLE DRILL
4:40 6	BPU <-----------------		RVA	<----------------------		BPU
4:50 7	LOVERS LANE <-----------------		OUTSIDE	<------------------------------		
5:00 8	TEAM VS DEFENSE <-------------------------------------					
5:10 9	TEAM VS DEFENSE <-------------------------------------					
10						
11						
12						
13						
14						

TEAM MEETING:

I. OVERALL A Good spring --- A good offseason ---

II. Not All problems solved
  1. Depth --- who else can help us win
  2. Passing game excellented
  3. Pass Rush --- who will get us pressure
  4. Kicking game --- can it be a difference maker for us

III. For every challenge = Opportunity

IV. Things are in place
  1. Exciting QB
  2. Exciting RB's
  3. Exciting OL
  4. Exciting LBers
  5. Potential in the front & secondary
  6. Great kicker
  7. Potential at punter better than we've ever had
  8. Coaches working hard
  9. Leadership growing in senior class

V. This summer is crucial
  1. Attitude
  2. Work ethic
  → 3. Bonding
  → 4. Trusting

CHAPTER • 3

Fall Practice

Pre-season practice always begins in early August. Our freshmen report a few days in advance of the upperclassmen, which gives both the coaches and the new players a chance to acclimate to one another. Some of the freshmen, and most of our veteran players, stayed on campus through the summer and worked out. I was really encouraged by the running and lifting guys were doing on their own throughout the summer. John Stucky counted seventy-five players lifting one day in the summer. I had told our players before we broke at the end of spring that we needed to be a team of workers and listeners, and that would make us winners this fall. Judging by their effort over the summer, they had both listened and worked. They gave both the team and their coaches a lot of confidence leading into the fall.

Our freshman class was a physically impressive group. They reported in shape and were eager to learn and to please. We had some linemen and defensive backs I thought could potentially help us this year. I would prefer to redshirt all our freshmen every year, but in today's world of reduced scholarships, that is impossible. After working the freshmen out in shorts and helmets for three days, I wasn't sure if any of them could have an impact this year, but I was certain that a bunch of them would have a huge impact on our program before their careers were over.

The veteran players were anxious to start practice. They knew a lot of fans and people that follow college football were pessimistic about their prospects this season. I'm convinced that's why we had such a good spring and summer—we had a team that wanted to prove the doubters wrong. With the exception of a player or two, our returning guys came to camp quicker and stronger than they had been the previous spring, and they were excited to prove themselves.

Our team did not have all of the problems solved when we reported in August. We had several areas that we needed to improve on from the spring in order to have a chance to defend our SEC championship. First, we had to have more depth: players who could give us fifteen or twenty snaps a game to keep our starters strong late in the game or who could step up when the guy in front of them was injured. We needed to accelerate our passing game from the spring. Tee had thrown a lot of passes to our receivers over the summer, and they needed to carry their improvement from the summer on through pre-season practice. We needed to improve our pass rush and have ten players up front who could put pressure on our opponent's quarterback. Finally, our kicking game, especially the punting, needed attention and improvement because that was an area that could be a positive difference maker for us this season.

> I told our team that for every great challenge there was an opportunity, and this team had an opportunity to be special.

I listed these challenges on the board to our team during our first team meeting in the fall. I told them that it all starts with the offensive and defensive lines and the linebackers and fullbacks. Those positions were the tempo setters and determined how physical our team was going to be. I told our team that for every great challenge there was an opportunity, and this team had an opportunity to be special. Their attitude and work ethic had been excellent, and the bonding and trust of one another made our team strong. I reminded them that it took every member of this team to contribute his part and that we had to depend on each other to do our part. The keys, I said, were preparation and passion in their play.

Our fall practices had lots of passionate play. Several players began to emerge as guys whom we could count on to help us. Guys in the secondary like Steve Johnson and Andre Lott, and linebackers like Judd Granzow and Chris Ramseur. Up front, DeAngelo Lloyd and Roger Alexander showed they could give us quality play. Freshmen like Bernard Jackson, Will Overstreet, Willie Miles, Tad Golden, and Teddy Gaines, all appeared as if they could provide much-needed help.

At wide receiver, Cedrick Wilson was rapidly improving and David Martin was showing the potential to really be a weapon. Mike Barry's troops up front were awfully solid looking, with Jarvis Reado and Josh Tucker showing they could be guys we could count on. Travis Henry and Travis Stephens impressed anybody who was paying attention on the practice field. Our depth was emerging.

The most positive thing about pre-season practice was how hard our players worked. I'm fond of an old Winchester (my Tennessee hometown) saying that says, "Most people miss seeing success because it's dressed in overalls and looks like work." Our football players were going to have success—it was just a matter of how much. The staff was working at a frantic pace trying to get everybody and everything ready for the season. It was lots of work, but we were all having fun. After about three weeks of hitting each other, though, our football team was hungry to play a game.

Our staff discussions about our early season philosophy and maximizing our strengths and minimizing our weaknesses against a very tough early season schedule were crucial. A "team attitude" was established and the discussions were great. Play tough, physical football, run the ball, stop the run, and win with defense and the kicking game as our young quarterback developed.

A crucial late, two-a-day decision to move Cosey Coleman to guard and Spencer Riley to center and start Jarvis Reado at right tackle was an extremely important factor. It took some unselfishness by a couple of proven players, as well as a tough call by the head coach and offensive staff. This move really solidified our offensive line.

I decided to put a ladder on the wall of our locker room and to place the name of each opponent on a rung of the ladder. I wanted our players to worry about climbing one rung at a time. The first rung was Syracuse.

CHAPTER • 4

Syracuse

If you are going to be the best, you've got to beat the best. That's what I said about opening our football season against highly regarded Big East power Syracuse at the Carrier Dome. I had first watched Syracuse some on film, shortly before spring practice. I watched them a lot during the summer and before our two-a-days started, and, boy, were they a scary team. Syracuse was easily the best team we had faced in an opening game in my head-coaching career.

Their quarterback, Donovan McNabb, was as good a combination thrower-runner as we had faced since I had been at Tennessee. On film, he was a bit inconsistent at times, but when he was on, he was as good as it gets. They had terrific speed at wideout, and one of their guys was an All-America. But I'll tell you what worried me the most about the Orangemen, was their getting their option game going and spreading us out a bit and turning over the game to their big fullback Rob Konrad. That guy is a heck of a football player and there was no inconsistency about him if they got you spread out.

Defensively, we really did not know what to expect from Syracuse. Of course, that presented a problem for us in not knowing how to attack them. Syracuse had brought back George DeLeone to their coaching staff as defensive coordinator from the National Football League after being a long-time offensive assistant there. George was a quality coach, and it was a little bit of a crapshoot in making our offensive preparations.

Every game in college football is important because you play so few of them. Unlike college basketball, where a season has thirty to thirty-five games and a tournament concludes your season, each college football game has special significance. The first can have even more significance because

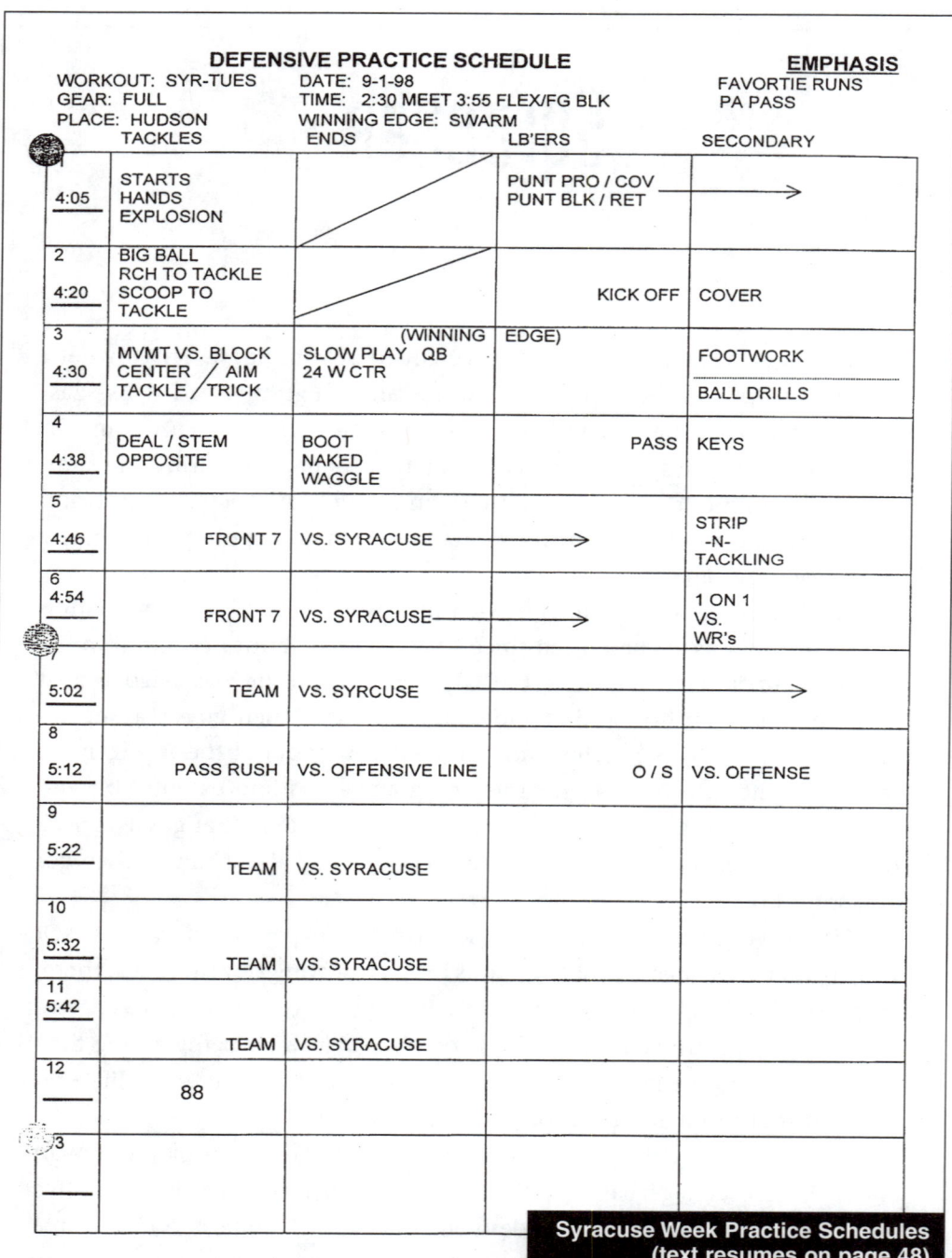

Syracuse Week Practice Schedules
(text resumes on page 48)

46 A PERFECT SEASON

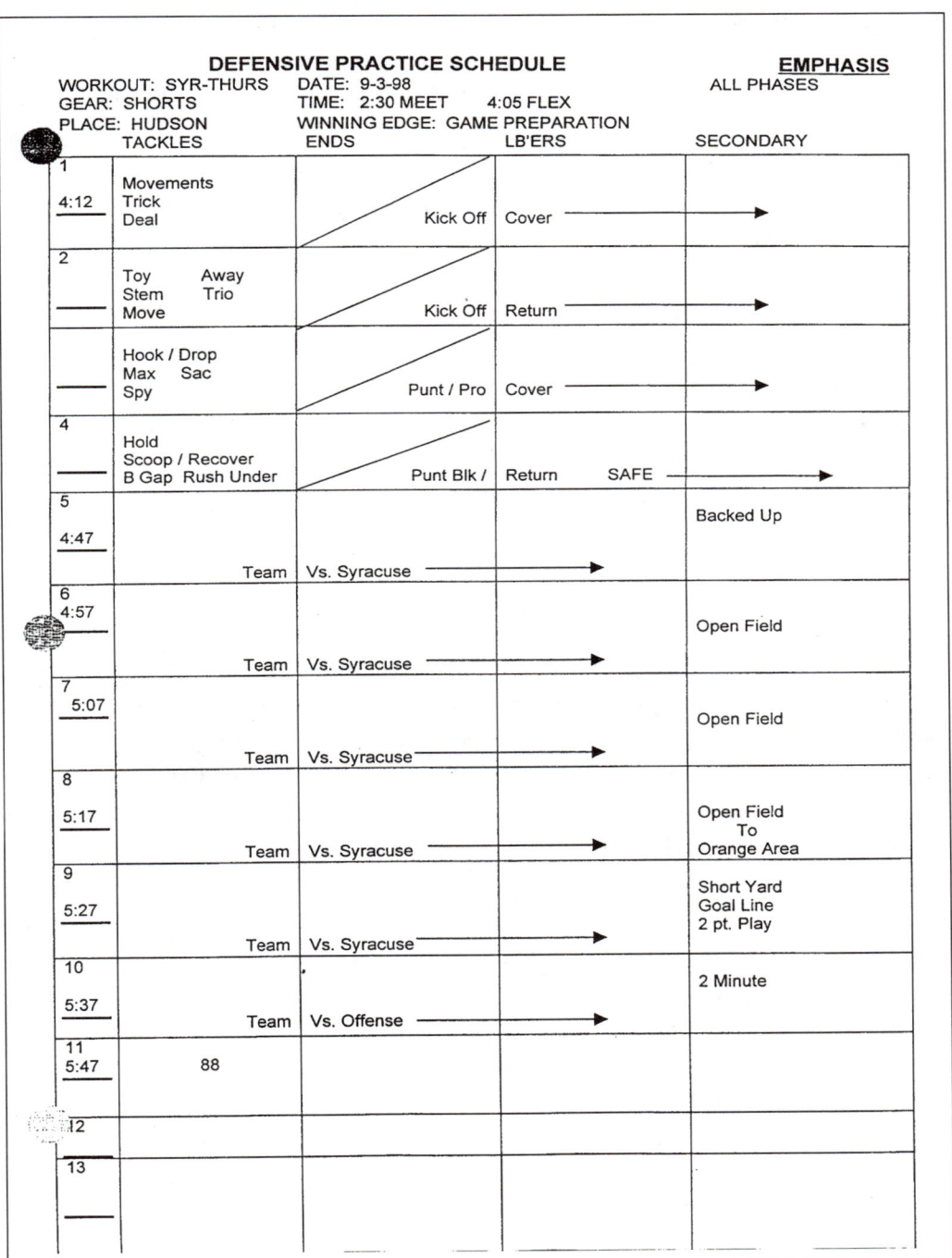

DEFENSIVE PRACTICE SCHEDULE   EMPHASIS

WORKOUT: SYR-THURS   DATE: 9-3-98   ALL PHASES
GEAR: SHORTS   TIME: 2:30 MEET   4:05 FLEX
PLACE: HUDSON   WINNING EDGE: GAME PREPARATION

# / Time	TACKLES	ENDS	LB'ERS	SECONDARY
1 — 4:12	Movements / Trick / Deal	Kick Off	Cover	→
2	Toy Away / Stem Trio / Move	Kick Off	Return	→
3	Hook / Drop / Max Sac / Spy	Punt / Pro	Cover	→
4	Hold / Scoop / Recover / B Gap Rush Under	Punt Blk /	Return SAFE	→
5 — 4:47		Team	Vs. Syracuse →	Backed Up
6 — 4:57		Team	Vs. Syracuse →	Open Field
7 — 5:07		Team	Vs. Syracuse →	Open Field
8 — 5:17		Team	Vs. Syracuse →	Open Field To Orange Area
9 — 5:27		Team	Vs. Syracuse →	Short Yard / Goal Line / 2 pt. Play
10 — 5:37		Team	Vs. Offense →	2 Minute
11 — 5:47	88			
12				
13				

SYRACUSE   47

it often sets the tone for the entire year. I viewed this opener with Syracuse as a *major* game. I thought the winner of this game would really put itself in a good position for the polls, bowls, and national prominence. This game was going to be on national television, and I sensed the nation would be watching us in our first "post-Peyton" game to see how we would respond.

Normally, the week before the opening game, you start putting together your game plan for your opponent. We started a couple of days earlier this year to get ready for Syracuse. Our staff, I'm sure like most every college staff, had looked at film on all of our opponents throughout the winter, spring, and summer. You want to get a feel for what teams do, take notes, and hopefully track tendencies through down and distance and formation. It would be impossible to try to look at game film for the first time of an opponent the week of the game and adequately prepare your game plan. For a team like Syracuse, you needed more time than you ever have.

> **I sensed the nation would be watching us in our first "post-Peyton" game to see how we would respond.**

Offensively, we had several key considerations for this game. First of all, we needed to get our new quarterback into the flow. It was important for Tee to have as much success as early as possible. Some early success was important, because I felt we had to score several touchdowns to win. Our offensive staff thought Syracuse would load up on the run, especially early, with an eight-man front to stop Jamal and our running game. So it was decided we would let Tee throw the ball down the field early in the game. Another key consideration was ball control. I didn't know how good Syracuse would be defensively, but no matter how good they would be on that side of the ball, we knew they would be better offensively. We had to keep their big-play people, their offensive guys, off the field as much as possible. When they did get the ball, it was also important for us to not give them a short field to work with.

Our offensive plan called for us to attempt right off the bat to stretch their defense by having Tee throw it downfield, and then give them a healthy dose of Jamal as the ball game went on. I believed our offensive line and running game could wear them down late in the game. Remember all the talk about being more physical that I had been saying earlier?

Defensively, our staff really had its work cut out. The decisions were a little like deciding which poison you were going to take. Playing against a team that runs the option means that your defensive players must be given assignments regarding which offensive man they are responsible for, and then be very disciplined to their assignments. An option football team is a difficult team to prepare for, especially when their quarterback is as big a threat as McNabb was. We stressed to our players in preparations the importance of being disciplined in their assignments against the option.

Syracuse threw the football more than just about any option team you'll ever see. It was clear that Syracuse was most dangerous when McNabb went back to throw and began to move a little bit. He's such a threat running that it makes your coverage people lose sight of the receivers while they worry about the quarterback. Invariably, the ball is thrown over your head to somebody who is lost in coverage and they get a touchdown on you. So, the keys for us were making McNabb pitch on the option and punish him with a good lick, and not losing containment on him in passing situations. We prepared for this by instructing our defensive ends to not ever let McNabb get outside of their rush and having Al Wilson "spy" on him in the middle. Our hope was that by making McNabb pitch on the option and then hitting him every time, two things would happen. One, we would be taking the football out of the hands of their best player, and two, that would then limit the effectiveness of their big fullback, Konrad.

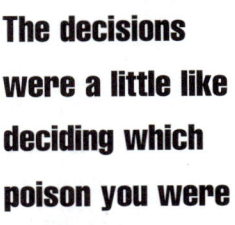

The decisions were a little like deciding which poison you were going to take.

Game week is dedicated strictly to your next opponent. In our meeting before this opening game, I stressed to our defensive unit the importance of their assignments and not losing containment. We told our corners and safeties that when the receivers broke off their routes, to not let them get behind the coverage. Our linebackers were preached to about staying in their lanes and keeping plays in front of them. We also told all of our defensive players they had to lock up on their tackles with Syracuse personnel, especially McNabb and Konrad. We decided to give a little cushion to Quinton Spotwood and Kevin Johnson on the outside because of their tremendous speed. More than anything else, we challenged our defense to be physical, to gang tackle, and to make McNabb beat us with his arm and not his feet.

In meetings with our offense, our staff repeatedly told our players to expect Syracuse to really challenge the run. We told them that we were going to continue to run, even if early on we were not having much success. That's because we felt the size and strength of our offensive line and backs would eventually wear them down. I told our offensive guys that, although I had all the confidence in the world in Tee and our passing game, we may at times struggle with that during the game. I further told them Tee was only going to get better and better, and we didn't just have to rely on him, but our success was just as dependent on the other ten guys as it was on the quarterback. I felt this approach was honest and took some pressure off Tee. He didn't lack confidence, but he was just about to go into a situation that the most adequate way to prepare for is game experience. Every meeting and every practice during this week with the offense began and ended with one thing: we must protect and not turn over the football.

We had installed our plans on both sides of the ball and on special teams, and we had practiced and met for a week preparing for Syracuse. Getting your players prepared for what happens when the whistle blows is just part of the battle. Another part with young players, especially, is preparing them for an environment like they have never experienced before. Our players already knew, or least they did by now, that Syracuse's home field was the Carrier Dome. It was my job to prepare and warn them about the loud and hostile arena they were about to enter.

I tried to do three things to help our players get ready for this: 1) we practiced some indoors with noise blaring to do our best to simulate some game situations where normal communications weren't possible; 2) we emphasized to our team that our eleven played their eleven, and the quietness or loudness of the crowd should not affect our effort; and 3) we met early in the week with our captains to encourage them to show leadership pre-game and during the game when the crowd got involved.

I guess I did a fourth thing in preparing our team for enemy territory. I told our guys in the locker room before the game that if they were the most physical team on the field, we'd never have to worry about their crowd because we'd never hear them.

When we arrived at Syracuse and went through our walk-through on Friday, I noticed a quiet confidence about our team. I had told them earlier in the week that we didn't have to be the best football team in the nation, we just had to be the best every Saturday we played. Our veterans, especially our captains, were really providing some leadership to our team, and our focus before this game was really encouraging to me.

Al Wilson, who is by far the best locker-room orator I've ever had, challenged his teammates and led us out of the locker room by saying, "This is just the start, baby."

At halftime of the game, with us ahead, 14-10, two things were on my mind. One, Syracuse was better than I thought they would be. McNabb was outstanding, and their defense was giving us a few more problems than I had anticipated. Two, I felt that if we kept from giving up big plays and held onto the football, our offensive line could wear them out late. I was concerned because McNabb was definitely on his game.

What a finish. Tee was terrific. Jamal ran with such force and strength. Our offensive line dominated late. Our receivers caught passes, protected the ball, and blocked well. Our senior co-captain kicker, Jeff Hall, nailed the winning field goal as the clock expired, giving us the 34-33 victory. Just another day at the office.

It was quite a locker-room scene. I was thrilled for Tee. I was happy for our team. They had met the challenge as the nation watched.

Our locker room was brimming with confidence. I didn't say a lot. I told our players that the most physical team had won, that they had showed great character in coming back in the last two and a half minutes, and that I felt our team had something special about them. We sang our Tennessee Victory Song, and I warned them about celebrating the win too long. We had just climbed, I told our team, one rung of the ladder. We all knew what was next.

CHAPTER • 5

Florida

I remember well the first spring and summer after being named head coach at Tennessee. It seemed as if everywhere that I went—and I went to a lot of places—all anyone ever wanted to talk about was "When are we going to beat Alabama?" I vividly remember one of my first speaking engagements after being named head coach, a sweet-looking, older lady came up and grabbed my hand and said, "Coach Fulmer, I don't care if you lose every doggone football game, I just want you to beat Alabama." Well, I guess if I saw that sweet lady last summer, she would have said the same thing—except she may have substituted Florida for Alabama.

Florida has probably become *the* game for Tennessee fans, much like Alabama was in the late eighties and early nineties. For the Tennessee coach, Florida has become a huge game for several obvious reasons. It's an early game; it involves an SEC Eastern Division opponent; and it's a game that affects not only the national rankings but national prestige as well. It is also a game in which, if you lose, the team that beats you must lose twice in the division for you to have a chance at the championship. That's usually not very likely. For less obvious reasons, it's become a very important game from my perspective. We recruit head to head against Florida for many of our players. We had also lost five straight games to Florida, and that's way too many.

Steve Spurrier has done an outstanding job at Florida since taking over that program. The first year I coached against him in 1992, we beat them. Since then, Florida had whitewashed us. As I look back at those ball games, except for 1994, when I thought they just physically manhandled us, we had committed the key turnovers, and they had capitalized on them. They have had some outstanding clubs, including their 1996 team that won the national championship.

DEFENSIVE PRACTICE SCHEDULE — EMPHASIS

WORKOUT: TUES (FLA)   DATE: 9-15-98   FAV RUNS / PA PASS
GEAR: VOL   TIME: 2:30 MEETING 4:05 FLEX/FG BLK
PLACE: HUDSON   WINNING EDGE: C M T

#	Time	TACKLES	ENDS	LB'ERS	SECONDARY
1	4:15	STARTS MOVEMENTS — BEAR / BASE √ CHANGE	PUNT / PUNT	PRO / COV BLK / RETURN	→
2	4:27	BLOCK REACT O / S TECH	HIP TECH 6 TECH LOCK OUT CHANGE STUNT	(WINNING EDGE) BOOTS & WAGGLE KEY	FOOTWORK FORMATION
3	4:35	I / S TECH LOW CUTOFF COMBOS	MOVEMENT "WASH" 2 ONE ONSIDE G ROLL	RUN KEY & SP DRAW ————————— PASS DROPS COV 8	ADJUSTMENTS
4	4:43	FRONT 7	VS. FLORIDA	→	1 ON 1 VS. DB'S
5	4:51	P.A. / HANDS FEET HIPS PASS / ACTIVE	P.A. PASS PASS RUSH	O /S VS.	OFFENSE
6	4:59	PASS RUSH	VS. OFF LINE	O / S VS.	FLORIDA
7	5:07	TEAM	VS. FLORIDA		
8	5:17	TEAM	VS. FLORIDA		
9	5:27	TEAM	VS. FLORIDA		
10	5:37	TEAM	VS. FLORIDA		
11	5:47	CONDITIONING		KICK OFF COVERAGE	
12	5:55	88			
13					

**Florida Week Practice Schedules
(text resumes on page 56)**

54   A PERFECT SEASON

DEFENSIVE PRACTICE SCHEDULE

WORKOUT: THUR (FLA)   **DATE:** 9-17-98
GEAR: SHORTS   **TIME:** 2:30 MEETING 4:05 FLEX
PLACE: HUDSON   **WINNING EDGE:** GAME PREPARATION

EMPHASIS
ALL PHASES

#	Time	TACKLES	ENDS	LB'ERS	SECONDARY
1	4:12	MOVMENTS / BEAR / CUB	KICK	OFF COVERAGE	
2		MAX / HOOK / DROP	KICK	OFF RETURN	
3		MOVE / STEM / HOOK	PUNT	PRO / COVER	
4		OFF ENDS & WILL / BEAR (HANDS UP)	PUNT	BLK / RET / SAFE	
5	4:47	TEAM	VS. FLORIDA		BACKED UP
6	4:57	TEAM	VS. FLORIDA		OPEN FIELD
7	5:07	TEAM	VS. FLORIDA		OPEN FIELD
8	5:17	TEAM	VS. FLORIDA		OPEN FIELD TO ORANGE AREA
9	5:27	TEAM	VS. FLORIDA		
10	5:37	TEAM	VS. OFFENSE		
11	5:47	88			
12					
13					

FLORIDA

It was late Saturday evening when our team arrived back home in Knoxville from Syracuse. It wasn't long after arriving that I was off to tape the coach's show with John Ward. Almost immediately after the show, I was already looking at tape of Florida. In my business, the celebrations of victories are short.

I've looked at a great deal of Florida tape the last several years. I was joking with David Cutcliffe the Sunday after Syracuse that those two linebackers, Mike Peterson and Johnny Rutledge, and that end Tim Beauchamp, had to have been playing for Florida since 1992.

There's an old coaches' saying that "The tape doesn't lie." The tape *doesn't* lie, and if you watched Florida on tape the last several years, you would have seen that they have consistently beaten people because they stop the run on defense, and offensively, they have been able to run the football when they needed to run.

If you watched Florida on tape the last several years, you would have seen that they have consistently beaten people because they stop the run on defense.

Although we had an off week after Syracuse, it was anything but an off week for our coaches. I planned our normal team meeting for Sunday night after the game and decided to give our players Monday and Tuesday off. We had played and beaten a very good team at their place the day before, but I liked the serious nature of our team as we met Sunday. I told them to rest up because the next game was bigger than the one we had just won. I told them I had watched Florida on film and they were good, but we could beat them if we prepared well and were physical enough in our play. Closing the meeting I said I'd see everybody at practice on Wednesday. A lot of the guys spent Monday and Tuesday watching film. It was obvious our team was developing a very strong work ethic.

Most of our coaches stayed late that Sunday night watching film. A big game does that to you. It doesn't make a difference if you have a week or a month to prepare, if you're a coach you always wish you had more time. My coordinators, David and John, had been with me for several years and both regularly burned the midnight oil with me.

I studied film on Florida for most of the week, looking at not only what they had done the previous game or in the previous season, but what they had done against us over the last few years. Joe Harrington did a great job cutting up the film for our whole staff, and we all pored over it.

What jumped out at me immediately on film was Florida's defensive front and linebackers. Watching this group on tape was really watching a lot of reruns, as Florida had basically the same front seven for the last three years. Their front four reminded me of the group in 1994 when they shut us out in Knoxville with Kevin Carter, Ellis Johnson, and that bunch. Their inside guys, Ed Chester and Reggie McGrew, both could stuff the run and rush the passer, and they were both playmakers. Their ends were big and had enough speed to get up field and cause you problems. Their inside guys were actually a little more dangerous than their outside guys.

Their front seven did jump out at you as you studied them, but the guy who stood out above everyone else in the whole group was their outside linebacker, Jevon Kearse. His combination of speed and range made him one of the best players we'd ever played against. He was definitely a guy we had to plan around some. Their other outside linebacker, Mike Peterson, was smaller but was very fast and made a lot of plays. Their "mike" linebacker, Johnny Rutledge, was not as fast as the other linebackers, but he still had plenty enough speed to play the middle very effectively.

Florida's secondary was not as experienced or as talented as its front seven, and that was quite evident on film. They had good players back there, but they did not have the dominating cover cornerbacks they had the last few seasons. This team had two new corners, with one of them, Tony George, having moved over from strong safety. Their free safety, Teako Brown, was an experienced guy who had made several big plays against us in previous years. So what we ended up facing was a secondary with three new position guys and a front that returned everybody. A great front can make your secondary a lot better, and I clearly saw that with Florida on film.

Looking at Florida offensively, I saw a lot of what I'd been seeing for years. Their offensive line was good, with their big left tackle, Zach Pillar, being an outstanding player. They had a tailback, Terry Jackson, who was really a good athlete and who seemingly had been around forever. He reminded me of a couple of the tailbacks Florida has had the last several years, Eric Rhett and Fred Taylor. Taylor was faster, but Jackson, like Rhett, could catch the ball awfully well.

Florida did not have a Jacquez Green, a Reidel Anthony, or an Ike Hilliard on this team, but they were really good at wideout. They had a little guy, Travis McGriff, out there, who reminded me of Green. Other guys showed up enough on film, like Taylor, to tell me they could beat you also if you weren't real careful. Florida had another wideout they signed, John Capel. I didn't see much of him on their film, but I had seen high school film of him enough to know we had better be aware of him if he's in the game because he has tremendous speed. He's like a guy we signed this year, Leonard Scott, from Louisiana.

Quarterback study of Florida was interesting because you were not sure who you were going to get. They had two guys who had both started, Doug Johnson and Jesse Palmer, and both were good players. Johnson had started the year before against us, but Palmer started Florida's opening game of 1998. There wasn't a lot of difference in them on film, except that you could tell Johnson had a little stronger arm. I really didn't care who we got but kind of hoped both would play a lot. The key to being effective defensively against their team is not controlled by who lines up under the center.

Special teams were a little mixed for Florida. Their punting was good, but their kicker was a little erratic. They were clearly dangerous in the return game on film.

Our practice was spirited throughout our open-date week. We worked on fundamentals early and then began on some work simulating Florida. By the end of the week, the excitement around campus and our community was extremely high. Our staff was preparing hard, and we were excited, too.

I told our staff every day in meetings that the way to beat Florida was to use the same recipe we had committed to last spring, which was to be more physical, run the football, and stop the run. We planned and schemed around that recipe.

How did we plan to attack them offensively? Well, they say history is the best teacher and the last few years we had not run the ball effectively against them. In this game we were going to run the football, and we were going to keep running the football.

Florida puts a lot of defenders in the box hoping to make it difficult for you to run on first down. They usually line up with eight defenders close to the line of scrimmage. If they hold you to little or no gain, or a loss, on first down, the natural tendency for the offense is to spread and throw. When you did that, Florida, wisely using its personnel, would often put Kearse at end and on obvious passing downs—he's a terror.

I believed that we ought to run it at them on first and second down, unless the down-and-distance call was unreasonable. My thinking was that by continuing to run, it would first of all put the ball more often into the hands of our biggest offensive threat, Jamal Lewis. Second, Jamal was a punishing runner, and I thought our offensive line would wear them down some late. Last, I wanted to take the physical fight to them, and you could do that best by running the ball.

We certainly didn't plan to abandon the pass and be one dimensional against this outstanding defense. David Cutcliffe had watched a ton of film on them and believed we could throw deep on them. Our offensive staff thought we could get a couple of scores by throwing over them because they played so much bump and run. We decided to let Tee throw the football down the field. Tee had not been as accurate as he could be at Syracuse, but he made the throws when we needed them. He had been throwing well in practice, especially the deep ball. David and his staff liked Peerless Price deep on whomever was on him.

Our offensive plan was pretty simple. We were going to run, control down and distance, and run mostly inside where our best run blocker, Cosey Coleman, played. We were going to continue to run, even when down and distance seemed to indicate pass. When we threw, we were going to throw downfield and over the top. We planned this way because we believed in our defense and felt like we had the advantage in the kicking game.

How did we prepare defensively? Florida has a reputation as a passing team, and they really lull people into not focusing on stopping the run. I knew that for us to win, we would have to limit their ability to run. Florida has done a good job under Coach Spurrier of taking what the defense would give them, and if you overcompensated in your package for the pass, they would run it at you. We were not going to let them run, even if that meant bringing our safeties up to the line of scrimmage. I felt like our base defense could stop them from running. I thought we were strong enough up the middle and fast enough at linebackers to get that done.

Our defense package has evolved under John Chavis and his staff to very much a pressure package. Against Florida, I didn't believe we ought to change one bit and, as a matter of fact, felt, if anything, we ought to turn it up a notch or two. John believed from watching on film that our quickness at linebacker would allow us to be effective with our blitz package.

Watching Florida to any degree on film or in person, you clearly see their passing game is based on timing. They do a very good job at this. We thought that by applying maximum pressure, we had the best chance to disrupt some of their timing patterns. Obviously, playing so much pressure defense puts a great burden on your secondary. We worked very hard in practice on technique and focused on making the tackle after the catch. Executing on the little things, like making a clean tackle after the catch, was a key to carrying out our defensive plans.

Our defensive coaches told their players all week in practice and in meetings that they would have lots of opportunities to create turnovers in this game. Players like quarterbacks and wide receivers who weren't used to running with the ball in traffic would have it in their hands a lot Saturday. They not only kept telling them that, they coached stripping and recovering the ball afterward.

Our players seemed to have a great weekend during the open date. Many of them watched Syracuse impressively whip Michigan Saturday, and a lot of them were around the football complex over the weekend. Our regular Sunday night team meeting was good. I didn't have to tell them anything special or act any different. They knew what was coming up at the end of the week. They were excited. Our staff was excited. I was excited.

We had a great week of practice. I could just see the leadership and character of our team growing. I'm not just talking about Al and the rest of the captains and seniors. I'm talking about guys like Tee, Jamal, Eric Westmoreland, Billy Ratliff, Cedrick Wilson, and others. These guys were encouragers, challengers—competitive guys who did their part and pushed others as well.

The start of the game Saturday was late so as to accommodate television. The stadium was beautiful *and* loud. During pre-game warm-ups, I remember thinking how poised and confident Tee seemed to be. I was more nervous than he was. I also remember Jeff Hall was kicking the heck out of the football. Our guys were unbelievably excited as we left the field to go back up into the tunnel right before kickoff, and I knew this game was going to be something special.

In the locker room, things were naturally quiet as we prayed and then I shared my thoughts with the team. I talked about doing the things we had worked on since the spring—being more physical, taking the fight to Florida, keeping our poise, and not turning over the football. Last, I told our team that I believed in them, that this is exactly what they had worked so hard for. The hours in the weight room, the extra sprints in the summer, the physical drills done in the hot two-a-day practices…this is why they came to Tennessee. I reminded them of keeping their poise, of playing for sixty minutes…one play at a time. I closed by telling them we would get the victory, because we were the best team.

During pre-game warm-ups, I remember thinking how poised and confident Tee seemed to be. I was more nervous than he was.

It was really, really quiet now and I asked if our captains wanted to say a word. Al Wilson stood up. Every eye in that locker room was on him. He said something like this: "I'm not walking off that field tonight without a win. Anybody that doesn't give it his all tonight has to answer to me." Al has the most unique way of connecting to guys I've ever seen. Coming out of the tunnel, our guys were juiced.

The game was full of big plays. The first one was Shawn Bryson's long touchdown run right up the middle. We all felt that Shawn could pop a long one if we caught Florida right. David caught them right, and Shawn showed his tremendous speed in outrunning the Florida secondary for the score.

Al Wilson caused Florida all kinds of problems and created huge turnovers. He had an extraordinary game. Raynoch Thompson was outstanding, as were Darwin Walker and Deon Grant. The strip of Terry Jackson in the end zone early was huge, and what a beautiful fourth-quarter interception Deon made. That was a grab for the ages. Tee again was big when he needed to be big. Poise…what about the run on third and long in overtime? Our offensive staff was right—Peerless beat two men and made a huge play for a touchdown reception.

FLORIDA   61

Jeff Hall again kicked the winning field goal, this time in overtime for a 20-17 victory over the Gators. A wild celebration ensued at the end. This Saturday really wasn't just another day at the office.

Our locker room was, well, just as you would expect. Amid all the hugs and shouts, I got our team's attention. I told them how proud I was of them, talked about our character and fight, and reminded them that this game was not the real prize. At that moment I'm not sure they believed me. The real prize as I told our team was what we did with the win over Florida. I made up my mind that we were going to keep getting better and, Houston, which had played UCLA very tough, was the team we were now focusing on.

We had not been a yo-yo team. I was very proud of our consistency of good play. We absolutely were not going to go anywhere but up, and absolutely we were not going to waste a great win over Florida by getting surprised by anyone the next week. If they were going to win, it was because they were better...not because we were still celebrating. We sang our Tennessee Victory Song and celebrated some more. These are the moments in life you want to bottle.

I left the stadium about two hours after the game to meet with family and a few friends. I was excited and I was relieved. That was a big win. We took a big step up the ladder.

CHAPTER • 6

Houston

You would think that after you opened your season by defeating two top-ten opponents, with one of them being your conference rival, a fellow could get a day off. Not a chance on a game week. In the world of Division I college football, it's a truth that you had better be ready every Saturday, because anybody can beat you nowadays. So barely eight hours after we celebrated our Florida victory in the locker room, our entire staff was back at work. We were getting ready for the Houston Cougars. I told our staff during the meeting Sunday that I really wasn't worried about our team "getting big-headed" or thinking it could just show up and win. Earlier I mentioned that our team was developing a strong work ethic, which all special teams have. I described our team during one of the media days as a "blue-collar team." Our guys kind of relished the moniker and rallied around it. When you combine a commitment to work with confident players and good leadership, you've got a championship combination. Our guys had that confidence, and I credit that to our coaching staff.

This is exactly what I told our players Monday afternoon during our team meeting. I didn't spend much time warning them about letdowns or losing focus, because I didn't detect one little bit that they were. I certainly did not feel after our Florida victory, or after our team meeting the next night, that our players were fully satisfied—only that they were satisfied *so far.*

As usual, we watched film on our next opponent—this time Houston—that Monday. It was evident that the Cougars did not possess the athletic ability or depth that our first two opponents had. They were, however, a well-coached football team with some skill guys who could really play. Kim Helton, their coach, had been a player for my coach and current boss,

HOUSTON   **OFFENSIVE PRACTICE SCHEDULE**
WORKOUT: #28   DATE: TUESDAY, SEPTEMBER 22, 1998
GEAR: FULL PADS   TIME: 2:30 MEET; 4:05 FLEX
PLACE: U.HUDSON   WINNING EDGE: POISE-NO TALK-NO SHOW

PER TIME	C-G	T	TE'S	WR	QB	RB
1 4:05	FLEX -->					
2 4:12	FG --->				Bags&Agilities Pass Wave Avoid Drill Footwork	FG
3 4:15	S/S BASE	POP & TURN REACH VS 2 MAN	PUNT S-S FINISH BOARDS	PUNT & PUNT RETURN	Warm Up Throw On Run Waggle Drill Sprint Drill Nakeds	PUNT & PUNT RETURN
4 4:27	<----------------------WINNING EDGE--------------------------> SCOOP VS FUNNELS TILT	HOOK SLED △ ------>		WARM UP BALL DRILL	T/A ------>	
5 4:35	MIDDLE DRILL ---------------------------->			RVA --------->		MIDDLE DRILL
6 4:43	BPU ------------------------------------>			1 ON 1 -------> VS DB's		BPU
7 4:51	LOVERS -------------> LANE		OUTSIDE VS HOUSTON ----------------->			
8 4:59	TEAM - PERIMETER --->					
9 5:07	PROTECTION ---------> REVIEW		OUTSIDE VS DEFENSE ------------------>			
10 5:17	TEAM - MIX --->					
11 5:27	TEAM - MIX --->					
12 5:37	TEAM VS DEFENSE -->					
13 5:47	KOC &	CONDITIONING				
14 5:55	88					

Houston Week Practice Schedules
(text resumes on page 68)

64   A PERFECT SEASON

Time to kick off the 1998 season. (UNIVERSITY OF TENNESSEE)

Syracuse quarterback Donovan McNabb could beat you in so many ways. (SYRACUSE UNIVERSITY ATHLETIC COMMUNICATIONS)

Syracuse fullback Rob Konrad also kept our hands full. (SYRACUSE UNIVERSITY ATHLETIC COMMUNICATIONS)

Welcome to Vol country! (UNIVERSITY OF TENNESSEE)

Tailback Jamal Lewis anchored our ground game against Florida. (TOM RAYMOND)

Smokey VIII, the latest in the line of blue ticks. (TOM RAYMOND)

Defensive tackle Jeff Coleman leaves his feet to knock a ball-toting Florida player off his. (TOM RAYMOND)

Tee Martin quickly opened his career as Tennessee's starting quarterback with strong tests against Syracuse and Florida, and he came through in flying colors. (TOM RAYMOND)

Jamal Lewis always draws a crowd against Florida. (TOM RAYMOND)

Linebacker Al Wilson was our most vocal leader, and his actions spoke volumes as well. (TOM RAYMOND)

The support of the Tennessee fans was terrific all season. (TOM RAYMOND)

Defensive back Deon Grant has a nice nose for the ball and had one of his five interceptions for the season against Florida. (TOM RAYMOND)

That's not Peyton Manning celebrating our victory over Florida, although there is a slight resemblance. (TOM RAYMOND)

Our kicker Jeff Hall is about to send one deep against Houston. (TOM RAYMOND)

The Pride of the Southland marching band. (TOM RAYMOND)

Jamal Lewis is off to the races against Houston. (Tom Raymond)

With Jamal Lewis soon to be out for the season with an injury, Travis Henry did a great job in helping to pick up the slack. (Tom Raymond)

A ball up for grabs against Houston. (TOM RAYMOND)

We had good pursuit against Houston. (TOM RAYMOND)

Auburn and Tennessee renewed an old rivalry. (COURTLAND RICHARDS PHOTO)

Shaun Ellis takes off with the ball against Auburn. (UNIVERSITY OF TENNESSEE)

Our punter David Leaverton works to put Auburn into a hole.
(COURTLAND RICHARDS PHOTO)

Linebacker Raynoch Thompson (46) is among those putting the hurt on an Auburn ballcarrier. (COURTLAND RICHARDS PHOTO)

DEFENSIVE PRACTICE SCHEDULE

WORKOUT: TUES (HOUS)   DATE: 9-22-98
GEAR: FULL   TIME: 2:30 MEETING 4:05 FLEX / FG BLK
PLACE: HUDSON   WINNING EDGE: FUNDAMENTALS

EMPHASIS
FAV. RUNS / PA PASS

# / Time	TACKLES	ENDS	LB'ERS	SECONDARY
1 / 4:05	TEAM	FLEX		
2 / 4:12	FG	BLOCK		
3 / 4:15	GET OFF (CHUTE) MVMTS (FREEZE) CHANGE DIRECT	PUNT PRO / PUNT BLOCK /	COVER RETURN	
4 / 4:27	HANDS EXPLOSION GET OFF / SHED	(WINNING TACKLE HIP TECH VS. OB WEAK	EDGE) W DRILL ANGLE TACKLE --------- BOOTS & WAGGLE	FOOTWORK --------- RELEASES
5 / 4:35	LOCKOUT TO TACKLE O/S I/S	COUNTER & BOOT	RUN KEYS	TACKLING --------- STRIP DRILL
6 / 4:43	FRONT 7	VS. HOUSTON		1 ON 1 VS. WR'S
7 / 4:51	PASS RUSH	VS. OFF. LINE	O/S	VS. HOUSTON
8 / 4:59	TEAM	VS. HOUSTON		
9 / 5:09	PASS RUSH TECH	PASS RUSH	O/S	VS. OFFENSE
10 / 5:17	TEAM	VS. HOUSTON		
11 / 5:27	TEAM	VS. HOUSTON		
12 / 5:37	TEAM	VS. OFFENSE		
13 / 5:47	CONDITIONING	KICK OFF COVERAGE		
14 / 5:55	88			

HOUSTON **OFFENSIVE PRACTICE SCHEDULE**
WORKOUT: #29   DATE: WEDNESDAY, SEPTEMBER 23, 1998
GEAR: VOL GEAR   TIME: 2:00 MEET; 3:45 FLEX
PLACE: U.HUDSON   WINNING EDGE: FG POOCH, QUICK KICK

PER TIME	C-G	T	TE'S	WR	QB	RB
1 3:45	FLEX -->					
2 3:55	S/S 2 MAN	BASE/HOOK	PUNT S&S BOARDS FINISH	PUNT & PUNT RETURN	POCKET MV. AVOID DR. FOOTWORK FAKE TEC	PUNT PUNT RETURN
3 4:07	SCOOP/ FUNNEL	SLIP'S P/Q	KOR ------------->		WARM UP PER.MECH. DROP&SHIFT THROWS	KOR
4 4:15	<--------------------------WINNING EDGE----------------------------> MIDDLE ---------------------------->			WARM UP BALL DRILL	MIDDLE --------> DRILL	
5 4:23	MIDDLE ----------------------------> DRILL			RVA ----------->		MIDDLE DRILL
6 4:31	BPU -------------->		ROUTE WORK BALL DRILLS	RVA ----------->		BPU
7 4:39	TWIST WORK ---------->		OUTSIDE VS HOUSTON ------------------->			
8 4:49	LOVERS --------------> LANE		OUTSIDE VS DEFENSE -------------------->			
9 4:57	TEAM - MIX --->					
10 5:07	TEAM - 3RD DOWNS -->					
11 5:17	TEAM - PERIMETER -->					
12 5:27	TEAM VS DEFENSE --->					
13 37	88					
14						

66   A PERFECT SEASON

DEFENSIVE PRACTICE SCHEDULE

EMPHASIS

WORKOUT: WED (HOUS) DATE: 9-23-98
GEAR: VOL TIME: 2:30 MEETING 3:45 FLEX
PLACE: HUDSON WINNING EDGE: 3RD DOWN CONVERSION

DB PASS, DRAW, SCREENS

#	Time	TACKLES	ENDS	LB'ERS	SECONDARY
1	3:45	TEAM	FLEX		
2	3:55	GET OFF (GO) CHUTE TACKLE QB LOW (BIG PAD)	PUNT / PUNT	PRO / COVER / BLK / RETURN	
3	4:07	MVMTS AIM MAX TOY ROCK LOW BLOCKER	KICK	OFF RETURN	
4	4:15	FLASH CTR LOW (CHUTE) UNDER TO OVER	(WINNING LOW BALL BEAR VS. CTR SKIN & COUNTER	EDGE) MAN PICK UPS	CRACK RUN SUPPORT
5	4:23	FRONT 7	VS. HOUSTON		FORMATION ADJUSTMENTS
6	4:31	PASS	RUSH GAMES	O/S	VS. HOUSTON
7	4:39	TEAM	VS. HOUSTON		
8	4:49	PASS RUSH	VS. OFF. LINE	O/S	VS. OFFENSE
9	4:57	TEAM	VS. HOUSTON		
10	5:07	TEAM	VS. HOUSTON		
11	5:17	TEAM	VS. HOUSTON		
12	5:27	TEAM	VS. OFFENSE		
13		88			
14					

Doug Dickey, and he was in the process of building their program back to the level it had been several years earlier.

Usually, when you come off such a big emotional victory over your rival, the next game is especially tough on a team. That gives your upcoming opponent an advantage. Fortunately for us, Houston had just played a very tough game of its own against UCLA, so I thought that, likewise, could potentially take a little bit out of them.

Offensively, Houston was well balanced, slightly favoring the pass. I thought their quarterback was a good player and they had ability outside. Their most dangerous player was their tailback, Ketric Sanford. He could take it to the barn on you.

Defensively, the mantra all week was "Don't let up."

Defensively, it looked like Houston had quality players but was a little short on depth. I respected how hard they played on both sides of the ball. I told our team that. For us, Tee Martin had made crucial plays to help us win our first two games. He had struggled a little bit, though, throwing the football, as he was 16 for 46 in his first two games. But that had been against high-quality competition, so we knew he was capable of much better numbers. In fact, Tee since the spring had been very accurate in throwing the football. In meeting with our offensive staff Monday, we all agreed to make it a priority to give Tee plenty of opportunities to throw.

Tee's confidence, mind you, wasn't descending. If anything he was more confident than when the season started. I just didn't want him to start looking at his numbers and having that affect his confidence. David talked to Tee some about the routes he felt most comfortable with, and we decided we were going to open things up some offensively. Tee loved hearing that, and we knew he would need it down the road.

Defensively, the mantra all week was "Don't let up." We wanted to contain Sanford as much as possible and bring lots of pressure on their quarterback. I felt like our speed on defense had a chance to really neutralize Houston.

Practices all week were strong. Our national ranking was much higher than it had been in pre-season, but I really didn't hear much talk about that around our team. However, when I stopped for gas or went to Cumberland

Avenue to pick up a sandwich, I heard a lot of talk about that. I thought by the end of the week we were ready to play well against Houston.

The game was an early evening contest. Tee was really crisp, as we completed 15 of 20 passes for 255 yards and won, 42-7. Jamal broke off a big run and was a force every time he touched the ball. Defensively, we really stopped their run and held them well throughout the game. Our effort was good. Lots of guys got to play, many for the first time. That was exciting.

We celebrated in the locker room. I'm not going to lie—we didn't celebrate as much as we had the week before. I spoke briefly, reminding our team that we had a tough league opponent coming up next. We sang our Tennessee Victory Song and I went home to be with my family. One more rung up the ladder. I liked where we were.

CHAPTER • 7

Auburn

I remember driving to the office the Sunday morning before this game thinking how things had really changed between these two old foes. We had a rivalry with Auburn, especially in the seventies and eighties, that produced some of the toughest and most physical games Tennessee played in that time span. When the SEC formed its East and West Divisions, this game dropped from an annual one to a rotating game.

This was to be our first game against Auburn since 1991. When we last played them, Pat Dye was their coach and they ran the football a great deal. Now Terry Bowden was at the helm, and they were throwing it a lot more. When we last played them, Bill Oliver was coordinating the defense over at Alabama. Now, Oliver was the defensive coordinator at Auburn, which is Alabama's bitter rival. Things had drastically changed at the place they call the "friendliest village on the plains." But to opponents, it's not so friendly.

As soon as I started looking at them on film, I saw one thing that hadn't changed a bit since 1991. Auburn was still playing tough, physical defense. They were talented on that side of the ball, and they were sound.

Bill Oliver has gained fame as an outstanding defensive coach, and rightly so. He and our offensive staff have been going at each other for several years now, and I knew going into this game that Oliver would absolutely have his troops ready. We had been on a pretty good roll against Oliver his last couple of years at Alabama, and our offense moved the ball and scored a lot of points against Auburn in last year's conference championship game. Knowing the competitor that Coach Oliver is, I anticipated Auburn's absolute best effort. We got it.

Defensively, they didn't have a guy like a Takeo Spikes who jumped right out at you. They just had a bunch of really good players who rarely

OFFENSIVE PRACTICE SCHEDULE

AUBURN
WORKOUT: #32 DATE: TUESDAY, SEPTEMBER 29, 1998
GEAR: PADS TIME: 2:30 MEET; 3:45 TO FIELD; 3:55 FLEX
PLACE: U. HUDSON WINNING EDGE: COVER RIGHT & LEFT

PER / TIME	C-G	T	TE'S	WR	QB	RB
1 / 3:55	FLEX -->					
2 / 4:02	F.G. --------------------------------->			WARM UP	BAGS-AGIL. PASS WAVE AVOID DRIL	----
3 / 4:05	S & S DOWN LINE ---------> 2 MAN HOOKS		PUNT & PUNT RETURN S&S/BOARDS	-------->	WARM UP OPT. PITCH PRESSURE THROWS THROWING	----- ON RUN
4 / 4:17	SCOOP ETHYL/ INSIDE	G/T RT SIDE G/T LT SIDE	HOOK SLED, RUB TRIANGLE	8/9 SLANT 2/3 EDGE W/MOTION	T/A -------->	
5 / 4:25	MIDDLE DRILL ------------------------>			RVA ---------->		MIDDLE DRILL
6 / 4:33	MIDDLE DRILL ------------------------>			RVA ---------->		MIDDLE DRILL
7 / 4:41	BPU -------------------------------->			1 ON 1 --------> VS DB's		BPU
8 / 4:49	PASS SETS ---------> RIP/CLUB/SPIN		OUTSIDE VS DEFENSE -------------------->			
9 / 4:57	TEAM - PERIMETER & QUICK GAME ------------------------------------>					
10 / 5:07	LOVERS -------------> LANE		OUTSIDE VS AUBURN --------------------->			
11 / 5:15	TEAM - MIX -->					
12 / 5:25	TEAM - MIX -->					
13 / 5:35	TEAM VS DEFENSE --->					
14 / 5:45	CONDITIONING & KOC					

Auburn Week Practice Schedules
(text resumes on page 76)

DEFENSIVE PRACTICE SCHEDULE

WORKOUT: TUES-AUB **DATE:** 9-29-98
GEAR: FULL **TIME:** 2:30 MTG, 3:55 FLEX
PLACE: HUDSON **WINNING EDGE: TEAM**

EMPHASIS
FAV RUNS / PA PASS

# / Time	TACKLES	ENDS	LB'ERS	SECONDARY
1 — 3:55	FLEX ————————————————————————→			
2 — 4:02	PAT/FG BLOCK ————————————————————→			
3 — 4:50	GET OFF / CHUTE / SHED BLOCK / MVMT/*CHUTE	PUNT / PUNT	PRO / COVER / BLK/RET	
4 — 5:17	HANDS / EXPLOSION / GET OFF SHED	(WINNING EDGE) SLEDWORK / MOVEMENT	W DRILL / ANGLE TACKLE / BOOTS & WAGGLE	FOOTWORK / TACKLING
5 — 4:25	TACKLE VS. REACH / ISO/TOSS / FAN ISO	HARD JOINT	TECH ————→	FADES/SLANTS / ←—— SEND SAFETY
6 — 4:33	FRONT 7	VS. AUBURN ————————→	←——	HANDS DRILLS / SAFTIES
7 — 4:41	FRONT 7	VS. AUBURN ————————→		1 ON 1 VS. WR'S
8 — 4:49	PASS RUSH / TECH / SWIPE ARM OFF	PASS RUSH SPEED	O/S	VS. OFFENSE
9 — 4:57	TEAM	VS. AUBURN		
10 — 5:07	PASS RUSH VS.	OFF LINE	O/S	VS. AUBURN
11 — 5:15	TEAM	VS. AUBURN		
12 — 5:25	TEAM	VS. AUBURN		
13 — 5:35	TEAM	VS. OFFENSE		
14 — 5:45	CONDITIONING/	KICK OFF COV.		

```
AUBURN                          OFFENSIVE PRACTICE SCHEDULE
WORKOUT: #34          DATE:  THURSDAY, OCTOBER 1, 1998
GEAR:  SHORTS         TIME:  2:30 MEET;3:40 FULMER;3:55 TO FIELD;4:05 FLEX
PLACE: U.HUDSON       WINNING EDGE: DRESS REHEARSAL
```

PER TIME	C-G	T	TE'S	WR	QB	RB
1 4:05	FLEX					
2 4:12	K.O.C.					
3	K.O.R.					
4	PUNT					
5	PUNT RETURN					
6 4:47	TEAM - G.L. 2 POINT PLAYS ---------------------------------->					
7 4:57	TEAM - BACKED UP - STALL - STORT YARDAGE ------------------>					
8 5:07	TEAM - ORANGE AREA - 3RD DOWNS ---------------------------->					
9 5:17	TEAM - PERIMETER - MIX ------------------------------------>					
10 5:27	TEAM - TAKE OFF --->					
11 5:37	2 MINUTE VS DEFENSE --------------------------------------->					
12 5:47	88					
13						
14						

A PERFECT SEASON

DEFENSIVE PRACTICE SCHEDULE

EMPHASIS

WORKOUT: THURS-AUB DATE: 10-01-98 ALL PHASES
GEAR: SHORTS TIME: 2:30 MTG, 4:05 FLEX
PLACE: HUDSON WINNING EDGE: **GAME PREPARATION**

#	TACKLES	ENDS	LB'ERS	SECONDARY
1 / 4:05	FLEX		→	
2 / 4:12	HOLD SPY PEEL	KICK	OFF COVERAGE	
3	MAX STAR EAGLE STAR DROP, HOOK	KICK	OFF RETURN	
4	STRESS WAC GAMES	PUNT	PRO/COVER	
5	SAFE TECH.	PUNT	BLK/RET/SAFE	
6 / 4:47	TEAM	VS. AUBURN		BACKED UP
7 / 4:57	TEAM	VS. AUBURN		OPEN FIELD
8 / 5:07	TEAM	VS. AUBURN		OPEN FIELD
9 / 5:17	TEAM	VS. AUBURN		OPEN FIELD TO ORANGE AREA
10 / 5:27	TEAM	VS. AUBURN		ORANGE AREA TO GOALLINE
11 / 5:37	TEAM	VS. OFFENSE		2 MINUTE
12 / 5:47	88			
13				
14				

AUBURN 75

were out of position to make a play. Their secondary was smart and they tackled exceptionally well.

Their front seven were not guys who were easily knocked off the ball. They had some players, like Leo Carson and Marcus Washington, who could penetrate and put you in a negative situation offensively.

On film it was quite evident that Auburn had been inconsistent on offense. They were having trouble running the football. Their offensive line had been besieged with injuries and guys leaving the program. They were also playing with a young quarterback, which can cause you some problems if you are not able to run the football like you want to run it.

I knew they had some real speed and ability outside, because Karsten Bailey was back. I saw enough of the young tailback, Michael Burks, to know they could potentially really get it going offensively if they got some confidence.

Their quarterback, Ben Leard, makes for an interesting "what if." I've mentioned earlier, and it's no secret, that we really recruited Tim Couch hard. We recruited Tim earlier, and initially harder, than any other quarterback in that class. You know the story; Couch commits to Kentucky, and there were basically two quarterbacks on our board that we had been recruiting—Ben Leard and Tee Martin. Ben was from Georgia and Tee from Mobile, an area that Auburn recruits heavily. Both young men visited both us and Auburn, and it was a fierce recruiting battle with Auburn for Tee. We were fortunate enough to sign Tee and Auburn was fortunate to sign Ben Leard. I think it's safe to say both would not have gone to the same school.

Speaking of Tee, our offensive unit was gaining confidence. The Houston game was big for Tee because he found such success throwing the ball, completing 14 of 19 passes for 234 yards. A quarterback is no different than any of the rest of us in our professions—the better we do, the more confident we feel.

David Cutcliffe and our offensive staff had spotted some things that we do that they thought gave us a chance to be really successful against Auburn's package, like the counter play to Jamal. We knew that we would really have to mix it up and be balanced offensively, or Auburn would catch our rhythm and disrupt it.

We planned to be physical, give them a healthy dose of Jamal on the counter trey and play it a little close to the vest. I didn't believe Auburn's defense could stop Jamal enough or their offense could score enough points against our defense to beat us.

Defensively, we wanted to control the line of scrimmage and stop the run and make them one-dimensional. We wanted to make their quarterback beat us. Again, I just believed Auburn would have a hard time scoring many points on our defense.

That's why all week long I stressed in our meetings and at practices the value of protecting the football. Of course, we always stress the importance of taking care of the ball, but there are some weeks that are more critical in doing that than others. This was one of those weeks.

Practice was good the entire week. I could tell our defense missed Al Wilson's leadership and tenacity. Al had separated his shoulder in the second quarter of the Houston game and would miss at least one game. I challenged Raynoch Thompson and Eric Westmoreland to step it up and pick up the load that Al carried for us. I thought they did that during the week and during the game, and I thought that Chris Ramseur played pretty well in there. You just don't replace an All-America middle linebacker and be the same. We weren't.

> One thing I didn't like about this game in front of us was that we were catching Auburn at a bad time.

One thing I didn't like about this game in front of us was that we were catching Auburn at a bad time. They needed a win. Their coach and program needed a win. They were at home and they have great tradition, so pride was on the line for them. I told our guys that in practice late in the week. I told them it would be a physical game, and the most physical team would win. I told them that I believed we were the better team, but this game could be won by the team that *wants* to win the most. Auburn was like an injured animal ready to fight for its life. It would take our best effort to win.

That was my challenge to our players. Be prepared for a battle. Don't expect Auburn to play like a team with a 1-3 record.

The game *was* a battle. They caught us early with a couple of option plays that we really didn't play well at all. Our big defensive end, Shaun Ellis, made a great play in intercepting a pitch and rambled about ninety yards for a touchdown. That was huge.

AUBURN   77

Let me digress from the game just a minute and say something about Shaun Ellis. Shaun is a talented young man from Anderson, South Carolina. Fortunately, he had picked us over Clemson, which is very near his home. Shaun was driving back to Knoxville from visiting home early last spring and fell asleep behind the wheel and had a terrible accident. I vividly remember going to see Shaun early the next morning after the accident and just how terrible he looked. To see this big, strapping athlete with cuts, lacerations, and serious injuries to his body was shocking. We weren't thinking about his football career; we were just praying he would heal to live a normal life. He shared with me some very personal thoughts, and his mom and I shed some tears. Shaun also told me to tell his teammates not to take the special gifts of life, school, and Tennessee football for granted. It can be gone in an instant.

In what I think is a great story about character and support, Shaun not only worked and trained to get back to a normal life, but worked and trained to resume his promising football career. I was so thrilled for Shaun as he was rambling, and I mean rambling down that field, because I knew what he had been through over those several months.

After Shaun's touchdown, we quickly got the ball back. Just as we had thought we would, we caught them on a misdirection cutback play, and Jamal took it sixty-seven yards for a touchdown. We got up on them early pretty good and not much else happened for us offensively the rest of the game. We did have one of the all-time-great, goal-line stands in which we held them four downs inside our one-yard line. That may have won the game.

We didn't protect the ball well, got out of synch offensively, and really kind of stunk the joint up for about two quarters offensively.

Early in the fourth quarter, a devastating thing happened to our team. Jamal Lewis suffered a season-ending knee injury. I knew it wasn't good by the way he limped off, but I honestly didn't believe it would end the season. I remember thinking as Jamal came off the field of a similar scene in 1990 against Pacific, when a great young running back named Chuck Webb limped off the field. I knew it may be trouble, but in my heart I just wasn't expecting what I got later.

We won this tough, physical game, 17-9. For the second week in a row, one of our best players had been injured. The locker room was happy but anxious. We all knew what Jamal and Al meant to our football team.

CHAPTER • 8

Georgia

The news about Jamal's knee late Saturday night was not good. Our medical staff told me that we would know for sure after an MRI, which would be performed Monday morning. I feared and suspected the worst—a season-ending injury. What a horrible time for Jamal and for our team to sustain this blow. I couldn't help but think of what I always told my players—that adversity creates opportunity, and toughness isn't well measured when everything is going your way. I was hurting for Jamal: He is such a special young man and a great competitor. I wish everyone knew him as we do—what a great personality and highly intelligent, hard-working person he is.

Our next game was certainly going to be a measure of our character and toughness. Georgia was coming into our game sky high. They had just beaten a highly ranked LSU team in Baton Rouge and were coming into the game ranked seventh in the nation and undefeated. On top of all that, we had beaten them seven straight times.

I sat alone in my office the morning after the Auburn game for a good while. While I knew Georgia would be a difficult opponent, I felt like I had to concentrate on the preparations of how best to handle our team and staff. I was confident by now that Jamal's injury, at a minimum, would make him unavailable for this game, and I was not optimistic that we would have Al Wilson at anywhere near full speed. My team was getting ready to play a crucial game of championship consequences without the services of our strongest offensive weapon and possibly without our best defensive player. My challenge was to buck up, go forward, be positive, and carry that kind of attitude to our staff meetings and our player meetings.

I met with David Cutcliffe and John Chavis and told them to start preparing their game plans without Jamal. We all thought that Travis Henry

GEORGIA   **OFFENSIVE PRACTICE SCHEDULE**
WORKOUT: #36   DATE: TUESDAY, OCTOBER 6, 1998
GEAR: FULL   TIME: 2:30 MEET; 3:55 FLEX
PLACE: U.HUDSON   WINNING EDGE: EXECUTION

PER TIME	C-G	T	TE'S	WR	QB	RB
1 3:55	FLEX -->					
2 4:02	FIELD GOAL -------------------->			S & S WARM UP	BAGS, AGIL. WARM UP CURL-FLAT	BAGS WARM UP
3 4:05	S&S DUCK 2 MAN	INSIDE FAN	PUNT ---------> PUNT RETURN		CORNER- FLAT QK THROWS	PUNT & PUNT RETURN
4 4:17	<------------------------WINNING EDGE------------------------------> P/Q SCOOP POP & TURN	RT & LT SLED/RUB/FAN	---------->	BALL DRILL ROUTE WORK	T/A --------->	
5 4:24	MIDDLE -----------------------------> DRILL			RVA ---------->		MIDDLE
6 4:31	MIDDLE -----------------------------> DRILL			RVA ---------->		MIDDLE
7 4:38	BPU - PLAY ACTION -------------->			1 ON 1 ---------> VS DB's		BPU
8 4:46	PASS SETS	TWISTS/SLANTS	OUTSIDE VS DEFENSE ------------------->			
9 4:54	TEAM - PERIMETER -->					
10 5:04	TEAM - PLAY ACTION -->					
11 5:14	LOVERS ------------> LANE		OUTSIDE VS GEORGIA ------------------->			
12 5:22	TEAM - 3WI -->					
13 5:32	TEAM - REG --->					
14 5:42	TEAM VS DEFENSE -->					
5:47	CONDITIONING					

Georgia Week Practice Schedules
(text resumes on page 84)

DEFENSIVE PRACTICE SCHEDULE

WORKOUT: TUE-GA **DATE:** 10-06-98
GEAR: FULL **TIME:** 2:30 MTG, 3:55 FLEX
PLACE: HUDSON **WINNING EDGE: EXECUTION**

EMPHASIS
FAV RUNS / PA PASS

#	TACKLES	ENDS	LB'ERS	SECONDARY
1 3:55	TEAM	FLEX		
2 4:02	PAT/	FG BLOCK		
3 4:05	STARTS (CHUTE) MVMT/BLOCKER PRESS UPFIELD	PUNT PUNT	PRO/COV BLK/RET	
4	HANDS | BIG EXPLOSION | BALL GETOFF	(WINNING TE MOTION FISH HOOK	EDGE) BOOT & WAGGLE KEY	FOOTWORK -------------- HANDS
5	TACKLING VS. BLOCK DWN/TRAP	MOVEMENT VS. SCHEME	MAN/MAN TECH PICK CALL COMBO CALL	TACKLING -------------- STRIP DRILL
6	FRONT 7	VS. GA RUNS		SAFETIES FORMATION ADJUSTMENTS
7	FRONT 7	VS. GA RUNS		1 VS. 1 WR'S
8	PASS RUSH TECH	PASS RUSH	O/S	VS. OFFENSE
9	TEAM	VS. GEORGIA		
10	TEAM	VS. GEORGIA		
11	PASS RUSH	VS. OFF. LINE	O/S	VS. GEORGIA
12	TEAM	VS. GEORGIA		
13	TEAM	VS. GEORGIA		
14	TEAM	VS. OFFENSE		
15	CONDITIONING/	KICK OFF COV		

GEORGIA

OFFENSIVE PRACTICE SCHEDULE

GEORGIA
WORKOUT: #38
GEAR: SHORTS
PLACE: U. HUDSON

DATE: THURSDAY, OCTOBER 8, 1998
TIME: 2:30 MEET; 3:40 FULMER; 3:55 FIELD; 4:05 FLEX
WINNING EDGE: DRESS REHEARSAL

TIME	C-G	T	TE'S	WR	QB	RB
1 4:05	FLEX --->					
2 4:12	KOC					
3	KOR					
4	PUNT					
5	PUNT RETURN					
6 4:47	TEAM - G.L.- 2 POINT PLAYS ----------------------------->					
7 4:57	TEAM - BACKED UP - STALL - SHORT YARDAGE ------------>					
8 5:07	TEAM - ORANGE AREA - 3RD DOWNS ---------------------->					
9 5:17	TEAM - PERIMETER - MIX ------------------------------->					
10 5:27	TEAM - TAKE OFF					
11 5:37	2 MINUTE DRILL					
12 5:47	88					
14						

82   A PERFECT SEASON

DEFENSIVE PRACTICE SCHEDULE

WORKOUT: THUR-GA   **DATE:** 10-08-98   **EMPHASIS**
GEAR: SHORTS   **TIME:** 2:30 MTG   ALL PHASES
PLACE: HUDSON   **WINNING EDGE:** GAME PREPARATION

#	Time	TACKLES	ENDS	LB'ERS	SECONDARY
1	4:05	TEAM	FLEX		
2	4:12	CUB WILLIE GO SCREEN CALL SPY/HOLD		KICK OFF COVERAGE	
3		HOOK DROP		KICK OFF RETURN	
4		LOW BLOCKS HANDS ON (LITTLE BALL)		PUNT PRO/COVER	
5		PUNT	BLOCK	RETURN	SAFE
6	4:47	TEAM	VS. GEORGIA		BACKED UP
7	4:57	TEAM	VS. GEORGIA		OPEN FIELD
8	5:07	TEAM	VS. GEORGIA		OPEN FIELD
9	5:17	TEAM	VS. GEORGIA		OPEN FIELD TO ORANGE AREA
10	5:27	TEAM	VS. GEORGIA		ORANGE AREA TO GOALLINE
11	5:37	TEAM	VS. OFFENSE		2 MINUTE
12	5:47	**88**			
13					
14					

and Travis Stephens would give us good play at tailback. We all knew that neither of them was Jamal Lewis, but together they could get it done. I also knew that Tee and the receivers would have to be a more important part of what we were doing—thank goodness we were on that track anyway from the Houston game on.

Georgia had two excellent offensive tackles and two really good tight ends. Champ Bailey gave them a tremendous weapon as wide receiver. With this package of offensive players, you can see how lethal they could be in the passing game. When Quincy Carter, their young quarterback, had time to relax in the pocket and throw the football, he was very accurate. It was also quite evident that if he saw open running lanes while sitting back in the pocket, he would tuck it in and run, as he was their second-leading rusher when we played them. I thought while watching film of their offense how much we needed Al Wilson. The Bulldogs' running game had not been as productive as their passing attack, but they didn't rely on it as much as they did their passing game.

Defensively, I thought Georgia had improved over the previous year (1997) on that side of the ball. Joe Kines, their defensive coordinator, is such a sound football coach; he always makes you work for every point you get against him. They had several good-looking defensive linemen that they interchanged. Their linebackers, especially Orantes Grant, could all run and make plays. Their secondary looked like a solid group except for Bailey, who was probably the best player in the country at his position or positions.

I told our entire staff Sunday night the key to this football game—we had to get after their quarterback. I knew it was feast or famine when you do that at times. I just felt that how we got after Carter would be the determining factor in this game. I know they had a chance to make some big plays on us if we kept the heat on, but I could live with that because I thought defensively we had a chance to make some big plays. I felt like we could pressure them up the middle with our blitz package. John and Steve Caldwell harped on our ends all week not to lose containment. It was important to not let Carter get outside of our ends when we sent pressure in the middle. Dan Brooks coached the tackle to get penetration and we could free whoever our middle linebacker was—hopefully, Al.

Against their defense, we had to pound it and make the game as physical as possible. Tee had to make some plays passing the ball, more than we did against Auburn, and he had to take care of the ball. I addressed our team for the first time after the Auburn game on Monday. After congratulating them on being 4-0 and the excellent effort they had given, I told them what our medical staff had told me earlier that afternoon—Jamal's knee had torn ligaments and he would be lost to us for the season. I immediately told our guys that others would have to step up and our team would have to rally around the loss of their teammate. I reminded them that they had met every challenge so far this year and had shown themselves to be tough-minded. That's what we ought to be; we're the defending SEC champion. At the end of the meeting, I told our team everybody was going to pick Georgia to beat us and that there was some talk that they were going to score fifty points on us. Our guys were wide-eyed when I said this, and I think a little steamed. They were hungry at practice Monday…and, as always, good listeners.

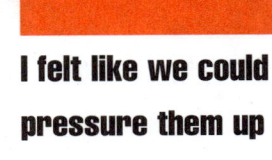

I felt like we could pressure them up the middle with our blitz package.

Our practices the entire week were good. Tee had an especially good week, which was encouraging because I felt we needed some big plays from him in Athens. The guys had bounced back from the loss of Jamal as well as I could have expected. As I've said before, there was a quiet confidence about this group.

Health-wise, Al Wilson practiced some this week and was going to try to return against Georgia. Unfortunately, his shoulder had the type of injury that could flare up with significant contact at any time. Al was hurting but going full blast, and our players took notice of that. Jamal's surgery went well, and a lot of us visited him at the hospital. I again saw a dynamic young man that I loved very much lying in a hospital bed. This was tough, but Jamal had his mom there, and, different from Shaun, we knew it was just a matter of time before he would be back with us. I told him how much I loved him. His mother, Mary, is a wonderful lady and a strength for us all.

Friday night, Coach Cutcliffe talked to the team using an analogy about the strength of the pack being in the wolf, and the strength of the wolf being in the pack. I thought it was particularly appropriate. In the locker room before the game, I followed up on that theme and told our guys that our team was a pack and a family, and there were a lot of wolves in the room. I said that our pack had met every challenge because we had refused to lose, and you do that because you have heart, character, mental toughness, and fight. Our pack was being challenged by Georgia, a team whose seniors have never beaten us, a team that says they want us badly. I called on our pack to respond to one more challenge and physically whip Georgia.

I finished my talk by saying that it would take sixty minutes of unbelievable effort to win, but the reward would be great. Our pack would be two games ahead in our division over Florida and Georgia. After I concluded, I looked around the locker room and I could tell our players were ready to play.

> **Our players had expected to win and were beginning to relish the idea of fooling the prognosticators.**

It was a beautiful day at Sanford Stadium. John Chavis had his defense ready and they got after Quincy Carter. Travis Stephens and Travis Henry stepped in for Jamal and both ran very well. Tee got our offense clicking toward the end of the second quarter, and it kept clicking until late in the game as we went on to win, 22-3. It was a total team victory and kept our winning streak over Georgia going.

After the game I looked for a gentleman who had stopped me before the game to tell me how they were going to escort me off the field for my safety when the fans rushed the field to tear the goalpost down. I couldn't find him anywhere.

The post-game locker room was electric. Our players had expected to win and were beginning to relish the idea of fooling the prognosticators. I told our guys how proud I was of them for carrying the fight to Georgia and preparing and playing with enthusiasm and intensity. I told them to celebrate but to remember our old rival, Alabama, was next. We sang our Tennessee Victory Song, and about an hour later we were on the plane headed back to Knoxville. One more rung up the ladder.

As I drove home from the airport Saturday night, I thought how this win would turn some heads nationally. We had just soundly beaten a very hot ball club at their home. Three times in five games we had beaten teams that the experts said we weren't suppose to beat. This was especially gratifying because it came on the heels of our losing a great player in Jamal Lewis. I knew I had a team of character—one that had a chance for greatness.

CHAPTER • 9

Alabama

It wasn't on the third Saturday in October, but to Tennessee fans the Alabama game is always special. We had been fortunate enough to have beaten Alabama the last three years. But when I go on the Big Orange Caravan or travel across the state, I still get a lot of "We've got to beat Alabama this year, Coach."

We had an open date before Alabama and I had mixed feelings about that. I was pleased to have a few extra days to get some of the guys who had been battling injuries, like Al Wilson and Fred White, a chance to rest and heal. But I hated to break the rhythm that I felt like our team was enjoying. Tee's comfort with our offense was really showing, and you could just see him getting better and better. Our two young tailbacks, Henry and Stephens, had just come off a strong game, and our offensive line was improving. And our defense was playing terrific. I gave our players Monday and Tuesday off from practice.

Our coaches were back to work the Sunday after Georgia. When you're winning, coming to the office every day is a whole lot more fun. For the first time, there was some talk around the coaches' offices about the Bowl Championship Series (B.C.S.). I was even a party to some of that with our coaches. However, I reminded every coach before they left the football complex that the only thing we could control was how we played, and the B.C.S., the polls, and the media we couldn't control. I had a feeling I might have the opportunity to say that a whole lot in the next month to our players. In the meantime, I had to worry about an improving Alabama team.

> **For the first time, there was some talk around the coaches' offices about the Bowl Championship Series.**

OPEN **OFFENSIVE PRACTICE SCHEDULE**
WORKOUT: #39   DATE: TUESDAY, OCTOBER 13, 1998
GEAR: VOL GEAR   TIME: 2:30 HEAD COACH;4:00 FLEX
PLACE: U.HUDSON   WINNING EDGE: FUNDAMENTALS

PER TIME	C-G	T	TE'S	WR	QB	RB
1 4:00	FLEX -->					
2 4:07	GAME MISTAKES	SLANT-P SLIP 4 I's-ODD 90-BACKSIDE PRO	S & S FOOTWORK	PUNT RETURN	DROPS-FOOTWORK BALL SEC. WARM UP	PUNT RETURN
3 4:13	GAME MISTAKES	60 ODD/BEAR RAMBO SLANT VS 42	BLOOPS KOR SQUIBS DECISION	KOR MAKING	THROWING ON RUN GUN QUICKS	KOR
4 4:19	INSIDE/ SCOOPS	POP & TURN (COWBOY)	RUB POP & TURN	PUSHING TECH BLOCKING ANGLES	PLAY ACT. FAKES & THROW SCRAM.DRILL	BALL SECURITY
5 4:27	BLOCK BACKS	POP & TURN (INDIAN)	FISH HOOKS SWEEP WORK	FINISH BLOCKS FINISHING ROUTES	T/A -------->	
6 4:35	MIDDLE DRILL ---------------------------->			RVA ---------->		MIDDLE DRILL
7 4:43	BPU ---------------> 60 660	ODD ------> BEAR	NAKED ROUTES NAKED RELEASES	1 ON 1 --------> VS DB's		BPU
8 4:51	PASS SETS	RIP/SLANT ---------> TWISTS E/T- T/E	OUTSIDE VS DEFENSE ------------------>			
9 4:59	TEAM - DBP VS DIFFERENT LOOKS ------------------------------------>					
10 5:09	TEAM - BASE RUNS VS LOOKS --->					
11 5:19	CONDITIONING					
12 5:30	88					
13						
14						

Alabama Week Practice Schedules
(text resumes on page 94)

DEFENSIVE PRACTICE SCHEDULE — EMPHASIS

WORKOUT: #2 OPEN DATE: 10-13-98
GEAR: VOL TIME: 2:30 MTG, 4:00 FLEX
PLACE: HUDSON WINNING EDGE: IMPROVEMENT

EMPHASIS: FUNDAMENTALS

# / Time	TACKLES	ENDS	LB'ERS	SECONDARY
1 — 4:00	TEAM	FLEX		
2 — 4:07	GET OFF / CHUTE MOVEMENTS	PUNT	RETURN	
3 — 4:13	REDIRCT / BEAR X / TWIST	KICK	OFF RETURN	
4 — 4:19	BLOCK REACT / HAT PLACE / HANDS O/S	(WINNING EDGE) CLOSE BACKSIDE 1. ZONE 2. NAKED	W-DRILL / MEDICINE BALL ---- IND CORRECTION	FOOTWORK & HANDS DRILL
5 — 4:27	I/S TECH / CUTOFF	CUT DRILL 1. TACKLE	↓	RELEASES FADE / SLANTS
6 — 4:35	COMBO'S / SCOOPS, PULLS	6 TECH 1. RUB 2. ZONE	PASS KEY ─────────────────→	
7 — 4:43	FRONT 7 VS. ALA	2 BACK RUNS ─────────→		1 ON 1 VS. WR'S
8 — 4:51	PASS RUSH TECH	CONE DRILL / UP FIELD / SHOULDER	O/S VS.	OFFENSE
9 — 4:59	TEAM	VS. ALABAMA		
10 — 5:09	TEAM	VS. ALABAMA		
11 — 5:17	TEAM	CONDITIONING		
12	**88**			
13				
14				

ALABAMA

OFFENSIVE PRACTICE SCHEDULE

ALABAMA
WORKOUT: #43
GEAR: FULL PADS
PLACE: U.HUDSON

DATE: TUESDAY, OCTOBER 20, 1998
TIME: 2:30 MEET; 3:55 FLEX; 5:55 88
WINNING EDGE: HANDLE PRESSURE

PER / TIME	C-G	T	TE'S	WR	QB	RB
1 / 3:55	FLEX -->					
2 / 4:02	FIELD GOAL ------------------------>		WARM UP	WARM UP / SHIFT DRILL / FLASH DRILL	F.G.
3 / 4:05	S/S 2 MAN POP & TURN	P SLIP	PUNT / PUNT RETURN ---------->		THROW ON RUN / BUCKET THROWS	PUNT & PUNT RETURN
4 / 4:17	INSIDE TATTOO	W/TE's HOOKS DIG OUT ------------>		BALL DRILL ROUTE WORK	T/A ---------->	
5 / 4:25	STAB DRILL G PULLS	W/TE's POP & TURN SLED ---------->		RVA ------------>		BALL SECURITY BLOCKING TECH
6 / 4:33	PERIMETER --->					
7 / 4:43	MIDDLE DRILL	M.DOG/MDX W/SHOOT/MLOOP	---------->	1 ON 1 ----------> W/DB'S		MIDDLE DRILL
8 / 4:51	BPU ------------------------------>			ROUTES VS ORANGE	SCOUTS AREA	BPU
9 / 4:59	TEAM - SHORT YARDAGE - BACKED UP - STALL ----------------------->					
10 / 5:09	TEAM - ORANGE AREA - PRESSURE ------------------------------>					
11 / 5:19	LOVERS LANE ------------>		OUTSIDE VS DEFENSE O/A ------------------->			
12 / 5:27	TEAM - MIX --->					
13 / 5:37	TEAM VS DEFENSE ------		PRESSURE ------------------>			
14 / 5:45	CONDITIONING					

DEFENSIVE PRACTICE SCHEDULE — EMPHASIS

WORKOUT: TUES-ALA **DATE:** 10-20-98 **FAV RUNS / PA PASS**
GEAR: FULL **TIME:** 2:30 MTG, 3:55 FLEX
PLACE: HUDSON **WINNING EDGE:** MIND SET / ATTITUDE

# / Time	TACKLES	ENDS	LB'ERS	SECONDARY
1 3:55	TEAM	FLEX		
2 4:02	PAT / FG	BLOCK		
3 4:05	GET OFF CHUTE BIG BALL MVMT/GO TO BALL	(FOOTWORK) PUNT PUNT BLK/	PRO / COVER RETURN	
4 4:17	HANDS EXPLOSION SEPARATE/ ESCAPE	(WINNING MOVEMENT TACKLE DROPS	EDGE) W DRILL PEEL OFF DRILL - - - - - - - - - - - SPOT DRILL	TACKLING STRIP DRILL
5 4:25	TACKLE OFF BLOCKER O/S TECH	CUT BLK BACK AWAY BOOT	BOOT & WAGGLE KEY - - - - - - - - - - - DRAW PASS KEY	3 RATT - - - - - - - - - KEY COVERAGE
6 4:33	I/S TECH REACTION BLOCKS	← FORMATION	ADJUSTMENT	→
7 4:43		FRONT 7	VS. BAMA RUNS →	1 ON 1 VS. WR'S
8 4:51		FRONT 7	VS. BAMA RUNS →	SEND SAFETIES FADE SLANTS
9 4:59	TEAM	VS. BAMA		
10 5:09	TEAM	VS. BAMA		
11 5:19	PASS RUSH	VS. OFF LINE	O/S VS.	OFFENSE
12 5:27	TEAM	VS. BAMA		
13 5:37	TEAM	VS. OFFENSE		
14 5:45	TEAM	CONDITIONING /	KICK OFF COV.	
15	88			

ALABAMA   91

```
ALABAMA                    OFFENSIVE PRACTICE SCHEDULE
WORKOUT: #45       DATE: THURSDAY, OCTOBER 22, 1998
GEAR:    SHORTS    TIME: 2:30 MEET;3:40 FULMER;4:05 FLEX
PLACE:   U.HUDSON  WINNING EDGE: DRESS REHEARSAL
```

PER TIME	C-G	T	TE'S	WR	QB	RB
1 4:05	FLEX -->					
2 4:12	KOC					
3	KOR					
4	PUNT					
5	PUNT RETURN					
6 4:47	TEAM - G.L. - 2 POINT PLAYS -------------------------->					
7 4:57	TEAM - BACKED UP - STALL - SHORT YARDAGE ------------>					
8 5:07	TEAM - ORANGE AREA - 3RD DOWNS ---------------------->					
9 5:17	TEAM - PERIMETER - MIX ------------------------------>					
10 5:27	TEAM - TAKE OFF ------------------------------------->					
11 5:37	2 MINUTE VS DEFENSE --------------------------------->					
12 5:47	88					
13						
14						

DEFENSIVE PRACTICE SCHEDULE   EMPHASIS

WORKOUT: THUR-ALA   DATE: 10-23-98   ALL PHASES
GEAR: SHORTS   TIME: 2:30 MTG, 4:05 FLEX
PLACE: HUDSON   WINNING EDGE: GAME PREPARATION

#	TACKLES	ENDS	LB'ERS	SECONDARY
1 4:05	TEAM	FLEX		
2 4:12	DROPS (#3) HOOK DROP OFF	KICK	OFF COVERAGE	
3	BEAR MAX	KICK	OFF RETURN	
4	SPY PEEL HOLD	PUNT	PRO/COVER	
5	PUNT	BLOCK	RET	SAFE
6 4:47	TEAM	VS. BAMA		BACKED UP
7 4:57	TEAM	VS. BAMA		OPEN FIELD
8 5:07	TEAM	VS. BAMA		OPEN FIELD
9 5:17	TEAM	VS. BAMA		OPEN FIELD TO ORANGE AREA
10 5:27	TEAM	VS. BAMA		ORANGE AREA TO GOALLINE
11 5:37	TEAM	VS. OFFENSE		2 MINUTE
12 5:47	88			
13				
14				
15				

ALABAMA   93

As I looked at Alabama on tape through our open week, I thought they were better offensively. They had a freshman quarterback, Andrew Zow, that reminded me some of Quincy Carter. Their tailback, Shaun Alexander, was an explosive player and one of the best players in our conference. They had skill at wide receiver with Michael Vaughn and Quincy Jackson, and their offensive line had been playing better.

It appeared to me that Zow added some excitement to their offense and gave opposing defenses a lot to worry about. Particularly, I was concerned about his ability to make plays with his scrambling. As a coach, there's nothing more scary than a quarterback who can take a play that's originally well defended, break out of the pocket, and create a play with his running or passing.

Defensively, Alabama played the same sort of pressure defense they have used for years. They give you a lot of different looks with their defense, so it was important for Tee and our offensive guys to spend a lot of time in film study.

Their defensive linemen were big and quick, with Kenny Smith being a player the offense always had to worry about. Alabama's linebackers were active and their secondary was talented, with an excellent cornerback in Fernando Bryant. As I mentioned, Alabama gave its opposition a lot of multiple looks to disguise which way they were going to bring pressure. Two things you could always count on playing against Alabama's defense: one, their corners would be in a lot of man coverage; and two, their safeties would cheat up to get involved in stopping your run.

Our team practiced three days during the open-date week and practiced well. Game week, I thought we stepped up our intensity a notch, which I expected, and I thought we practiced particularly well. One of the things that impressed me about our team was how well they listened. For instance, if we told our defensive ends to really be careful about containment when a quarterback scrambled—they did. This group was extremely coachable, and I told them early in the week of this game that they must continue that trait to make something really special happen.

In preparing for Alabama, John Chavis worked extra hard on our scramble drill in practice. I believed we would be able to pressure Zow, but I thought it vital that we make the scramble a bad play for them and not a good play. It was important that our defensive linemen stay in their lanes and linebackers close and tackle decisively in the open field. We, of course, played to try to shut down their running game and I felt like we could if we tackled well. Alexander was big and slippery, so when we got penetration we needed to pop him and wrap him up. I believed if we could limit their yardage when Zow scrambled and tackle well, we would prevail against their offense.

On offense, I told our guys that if we handled their multiple sets and were the most physical team, we could control the game offensively. I just thought we could run it on them, and get them cheating up so much that we could break a big play or two in the passing game on them.

I talked to the captains and the Unity Council during game week and reminded them to talk to their teammates about the history of this series and our great rivalry with Alabama. Some of the younger guys on our team really didn't know anything about this series, and I wanted them to hear it from the veteran players on the team. During our last team meeting before the game, I spoke to our players about the importance of this game. I briefly mentioned the rivalry and then talked about how this old foe would like nothing better than to ruin our unbeaten record. I said that the Alabama program needed a big win like this, and they would come in primed and ready for the upset. I closed by saying that if we let Alabama beat us—it would be because they wanted it more and not because the best team won.

Let me digress a minute and share with you two things that motivated our team not only this week but throughout the entire season. One involved Al Brown. Al and I have been good friends for several years. He's an assistant coach with the Lady Vols basketball program and outside of being a bad card player, he's a great guy. On several occasions, I've had the opportunity to talk philosophy with him. If you're a coach, you're a coach, and Al understands winning, he understands coaching, and I enjoyed our discussions as we traveled around on the Big Orange Caravan.

I will talk football or athletics with anyone I think can help. I've spent several quality hours with Pat Summitt, whom I admire and respect, and what coach has won more than she has? I've talked hours and hours with David Cutcliffe, John Chavis, and our other coaches when we travel together recruiting, or as we plan our attack for the year, or a particular week. I love listening to older coaches, younger coaches, pro coaches, or outstanding high school coaches talk philosophy or schemes as they look for their winning edge.

Anyway, back to Al. I asked him to come out and watch some of our two-a-day practices. I wanted to see what he thought about our organization, our tempo, our use of personnel, etc. He agreed and was out at practice every day. This was really good and I enjoyed his critiques, constructive criticism, and ideas. It was an unbiased opinion from a friend who knew about winning. We shared some great thoughts from time to time, most of the time in support of what we were doing, but occasionally he gave a fresh look at our program.

I've had other people I like and trust from whom I have solicited input, such as Doug Mathews, Coach Dickey, Charlie Coffey, visiting pro or college coaches, players, and anyone I think would know and care about our program. But Al was there every day and there were notes from him on my desk the next day. It was special.

I had asked Al to speak to the team as we approached the Florida game and he had done a nice job. He talked about how the Lady Vols had represented us as champions; how the SEC was chasing us and how if we played to our ability we would win the game. The players enjoyed the fresh voice speaking to them, and I followed the theme as the week went on. Al probably spoke to the team three or four times during the year, at my request, and each big game we won. It had become a tradition for the kids to look for him on big games and I was grateful. His basketball season had started so he couldn't be there as much, but his input remained as important to me as the counsel from my usual friends and advisors.

The second motivating factor involved my good friend Tom Ogle. Tom sent me a beautiful walking stick the week of the Alabama game. I love to hike in the mountains and this walking stick was carved beautifully with my name and "Tennessee Vols" on it. I took the stick to the practice field with me, I guess, just to show the players and as a conversation piece.

The players got a kick out of it, and they said I looked like Moses walking around with the stick. I didn't know exactly what to think of that, so I quickly gave the stick to my manager, Gerald Harrison, and told him to put it up. It was time to start preparing for Alabama. That night it hit me. *Moses.*

Moses had led his people to the Promised Land. I realized I had an opportunity here. So I called Al and asked him what he thought of my idea, and he gave me support to do it. It seemed a little crazy, but we needed a charge for the run during the last half of the season.

I brought all the team into our meeting room and put the whole room of chairs in a circle. I asked the seniors and captains to sit up front. I said, "OK, you guys called me Moses yesterday and had some fun with my stick. This is what we are going to do.

"It is going to take great energy for us to go through the season undefeated. It's got to take focus and concentration along with great effort. This stick is going to be your focus. Moses led the people to the Promised Land, and I'm going to lead you to an undefeated season.

"I'm standing in the center of this circle and this stick is in the center. Our energy is directed to the center of this room and therefore to this stick. This is now our Synergy Stick. When you see this stick on the practice field, in your meeting room, in the dressing room before the game, or on the sideline during the game, this is to remind you of the synergy (the focus of our energy) to win the game. It will recharge you and refocus you and your group to give our best effort."

The players got a kick out of it, and they said I looked like Moses walking around with the stick.

I passed the stick to Al Wilson. "Al, you take this. As our captain, you keep it with the linebackers today, then Mercedes will take it with the offensive line and we will pass it through the team."

I told our team, "You can't tell anyone what this is. It is just for us. Can't tell your girlfriend, your parents, the media, no one. This synergy is not to be shared."

By this time I'm thinking, "Is this corny or what?" But the main thing was, I was very sincere and they were very sincere in meeting our challenges. The stick was a great way to focus our team on the task at hand, and when they were in need of a boost…the stick and the synergy were always there.

Al took the stick and the rest is history.

We had the ability and now we were refocused.

That stick went everywhere. Team meetings, individual meetings, practice field, and it was the first thing that entered the bus and the last thing off the bus when we traveled. One player carried it with pride and our players made it work.

Moses was going to the Promised Land. I knew then that we would win them all. And that meant starting with our next game, against Alabama.

I am going to talk about a play during the Alabama game that most of you probably don't remember. But I thought it was one of the two biggest plays in the game; possibly one of the biggest in our season. Toward the middle of the game, we had the ball near midfield with fourth down and about a yard to go. I felt like our team at this juncture of the game was losing the momentum, so I went for it. Now mind you, going for it at this time, with this down and distance, was against my nature. Fortunately, we made it and won the game. If they had stopped us and had won the game, I would have been blistered for that call. After the game that play was mostly forgotten, but I felt like that play and Peerless's touchdown on the kickoff return were the two pivotal plays in the game.

We didn't play our best game against Alabama, and they probably didn't play their best against us. We played well enough to win, 35-18. Peerless Price's return after their third-quarter score was a dramatic shift in the game. Defensively, except for the one long touchdown run by Alexander, we played them pretty tough. Offensively, we were a little out of rhythm, but Alabama deserved some credit for that.

Rivalry games are hard to win. Oftentimes records don't count and you get the very best effort from your opponent. I was really pleased to have climbed this rung and so was our team. The air in the locker room was thick with excitement, as we had just won our fourth straight conference game and fourth straight over Alabama. Tennessee players and coaches especially love to sing the Tennessee Victory Song after beating Alabama. We were 6-0 and had just gotten through a tough stretch.

CHAPTER • 10

South Carolina

Our football team was undefeated going into the last game of October, which was on the road at South Carolina. I could see and hear the media already talking about the Arkansas game, which was nearly three weeks away. Arkansas, like us, was undefeated, and they would be favored in the games they played leading up to us. This kind of talk caused me concern, because we had two games we had to play before we faced Arkansas.

I told our staff Sunday after the Alabama victory that if we succeeded in anything as a staff the rest of the year, let's succeed in only worrying about the *next* game. As soon as I congratulated our players Monday for their effort against Alabama, I went straight to addressing my concerns about facing the task at hand. I told them that the task at hand wasn't worrying about the polls or the bowls or Arkansas or anybody else. The team had not given me any indications that they were doing that, or that they had lost any focus, period. I wanted to nip that in the bud. Our task at hand was South Carolina.

South Carolina had struggled so far this year. Brad Scott, one of the nicest men in our profession, had really been hit with a lot of injuries to his team. Their fine quarterback, Anthony Wright, appeared to still be suffering some from the terrible knee injury he had received at our game in Knoxville the year before. Their running game had not been a source of strength for them, either. Defensively, they really had a bunch of injuries and lost their outstanding safety, Arturo Freeman, who was probably their best defensive player, to a serious knee injury before the season started.

I had concerns about playing the Gamecocks, though, and I told our team what these were. I was concerned about their getting it going with their passing game, which they had the ability and propensity to do. I was also concerned about the hot weather. No matter how physically fit your

SOUTH CAROLINA **OFFENSIVE PRACTICE SCHEDULE**
WORKOUT: #47   DATE: TUESDAY, OCTOBER 27, 1998
GEAR: FULL PADS   TIME: 2:30 MEET; 3:55 FLEX
PLACE: U.HUDSON   WINNING EDGE: LEVERAGE & INTIMIDATION

PER/TIME	C-G	T	TE'S	WR	QB	RB
1 3:55	FLEX -->					
2 4:02	FIELD GOAL --------------------->			WARM UP	AGILITIES FOOTWORK- PLAY ACTION WARM UP	F.G.
3 4:05	S/S 2 MAN EVEN/INSIDE	POP & TURN INDIAN	PUNT --------> PUNT RETURN		THROW ON RUN GUN QUICKS SHIFT DRILL	PUNT P.R.
4 4:17	8/9 BOSS -------------------------------------->	Y BLOCK		ROUTE WORK BALL DRILL	T/A -------->	
5 4:25	MIDDLE ---------------------------------------> DRILL				RVA ------------>	MIDDLE DRILL
6 4:33	PERIMETER --->					
7 4:43	BPU -------------->			MAX WAGGLE RAMBO SLANT RAQ GAP	1 ON 1 -----------> VS DB'S	BPU
8 4:51	70 90 SHOOT 90 ---------> WAGGLE		OUTSIDE VS USC ---------------------->			
9 4:59	TEAM - RUN MIX --->					
10 5:09	TEAM - PLAY ACTION -->					
11 5:19	LOVERS -------------> LANE		OUTSIDE VS DEFENSE ------------------->			
12 5:27	TEAM - QUICK GAME - RUN MIX ------------------------------>					
13 5:37	TEAM VS DEFENSE -->					
14 5:45	CONDITIONING					

South Carolina Week Practice Schedules
(text resumes on page 104)

100   A PERFECT SEASON

DEFENSIVE PRACTICE SCHEDULE

WORKOUT: TUES S.CARL **DATE:** 10-27-98
GEAR: FULL **TIME:** 2:30 MTG 3:55 FLEX
PLACE: U HUDSON **WINNING EDGE:** CMT

EMPHASIS
FAVORITE RUNS / PA PASS

# / Time	TACKLES	ENDS	LB'ERS	SECONDARY
1 / 3:55	TEAM	FLEX		
2 / 4:02	PAT /	FG BLOCK		
3 / 4:05	GET OFF(CHUTE) MOVEMENTS	PUNT / PUNT	PRO/COV BLOCK/RET	
4 / 4:17	BLOCKER/SEP & TACKLE LOW BLOCKER	WINNING TACKLE TATOO/LB	EDGE W.DRILL/TACKLE TATOO WORK / END	FOOTWORK & BALL DRILLS
5 / 4:25	BLOCK REACT TRAP/BELLY	PWO- BELLY G BOOT – G PULL	BOOT & WAGGLE KEY -------- FLOW RULE	TWIN PASSING -------- PICK UP CUB BEAR
6 / 4:33	TEAM	VS. CAROLINA		
7 / 4:43	FRONT 7	VS. CAROLINA		1 ON 1 VS WRs
8 / 4:51	PASS RUSH PA SLANT TO TACKLE COME OFF	PASS RUSH PA SPRINT OUT	O/S VS	CAROLINA
9 / 4:59	TEAM	VS. CAROLINA		
10 / 5:09	PASS RUSH	VS. OFF. LINE	O/S	VS. OFFENSE
11 / 5:19	TEAM	VS. CAROLINA		
12 / 5:27	TEAM	VS. CAROLINA		
13 / 5:37	TEAM	VS. OFFENSE		
14 / 5:45	CONDTIONING/	KICK COVERAGE		
15	88			

SOUTH CAROLINA

SOUTH CAROLINA   **OFFENSIVE PRACTICE SCHEDULE**
WORKOUT: #49   DATE: THURSDAY, OCTOBER 29, 1998
GEAR: SHORTS   TIME: 2:00 MEET; 3:40 HEAD COACH; 4:05 FLEX
PLACE: U. HUDSON   WINNING EDGE: DRESS REHEARSAL

PER / TIME	C-G	T	TE'S	WR	QB	RB
1 / 4:05	FLEX -->					
2 / 4:12	KOC					
3	KOR					
4	PUNT					
5	PUNT RETURN					
6 / 4:47	TEAM - G.L. - 2 POINT PLAYS ---------------------->					
7 / 4:57	TEAM - BACKED UP - STALL - SHORT YARDAGE ------->					
8 / 5:07	TEAM - ORANGE AREA - 3RD DOWNS ------------------->					
9 / 5:17	TEAM - PERIMETER - MIX --------------------------->					
10 / 5:27	TEAM - TAKE OFF --------------------------------->					
11 / 5:37	2 MINUTE VS DEFENSE ----------------------------->					
12 / 5:47	88					
13						
14						

DEFENSIVE PRACTICE SCHEDULE   **EMPHASIS**

WORKOUT: THUR-S.CAR   DATE: 10-29-98   ALL PHASES
GEAR: SHORTS   TIME: 2:30 MTG, 4:05 FLEX
PLACE: HUDSON   WINNING EDGE: GAME PREPARATION
           TACKLES   ENDS   LB'ERS   SECONDARY

# / Time	TACKLES	ENDS	LB'ERS	SECONDARY
1 / 4:05	TEAM	FLEX		
2 / 4:12	DROPS / HOOK OFF	KICK	OFF COVERAGE	
3	GAMES CUB MIKE SHOOT	KICK	OFF RETURN	
4	MAX	PUNT	PRO/COVER	
5	PUNT	BLOCK	RET	SAFE
6 / 4:47	TEAM	VS. CAROLINA		BACKED UP
7 / 4:57	TEAM	VS. CAROLINA		OPEN FIELD
8 / 5:07	TEAM	VS. CAROLINA		OPEN FIELD
9 / 5:17	TEAM	VS. CAROLINA		OPEN FIELD TO ORANGE AREA
10 / 5:27	TEAM	VS. CARLOINA		ORANGE AREA
11 / 5:37	TEAM	VS. OFFENSE		2 MINUTE
12 / 5:47	88			
13				
14				
15				

team is, you just can't simulate the extreme heat or the extreme cold that you face if you travel to play a team with a different climate than yours. Finally, because we were undefeated and so highly ranked, a victory over us could make a team's season or change the direction of a program. That made us a big target to shoot at. I told our guys we were going to get everybody's "A" game, and we must practice and prepare for that. This was especially true against a team like South Carolina, which was playing at home and desperate for a victory.

Looking at their offense on film, I was really impressed by their skill at wide receiver. If they were going to give us trouble, I felt it would be in getting the ball to these talented receivers. If Wright got hot, I knew they could score some points. Offensively, I felt we could exploit their defense with our passing game. Tee had really been throwing the football well in practice.

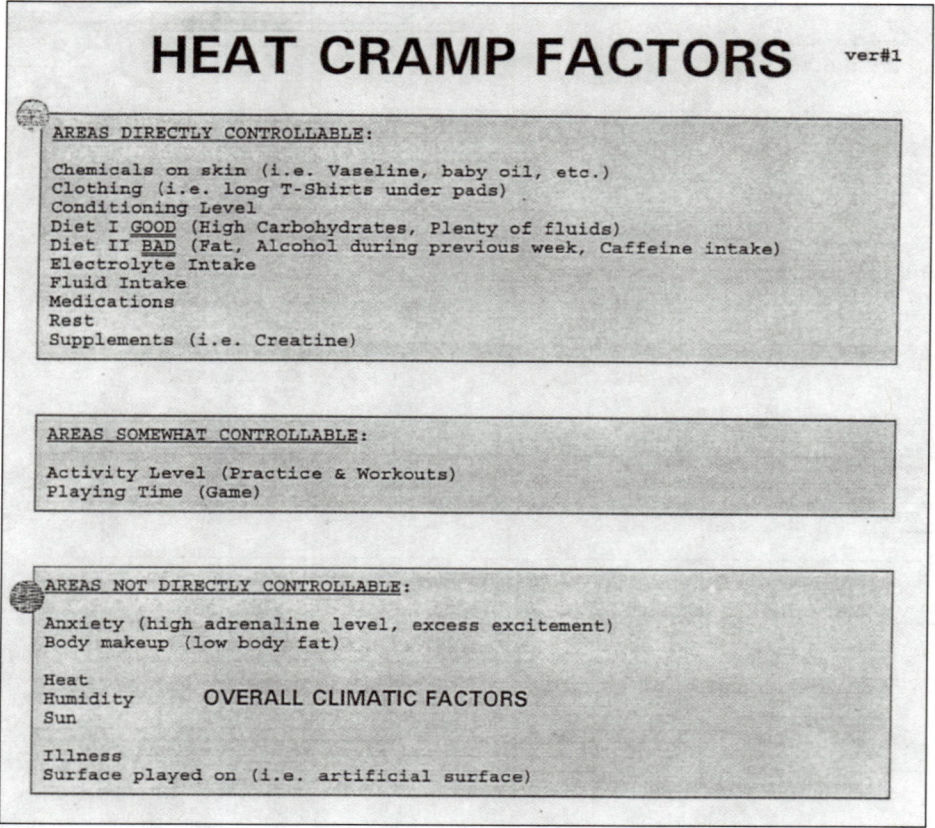

104   A PERFECT SEASON

Our practices all week were brisk and efficient. We were throwing and catching the ball well. We planned not to divert from what we had been doing defensively, which always meant bringing lots of pressure. I did not think South Carolina could run the football much against us. We surely didn't want Wright to have much time to deliver the football, so we intended to keep the pressure coming. I thought this was the only way they could beat us—by stopping our pressure and being very efficient in their passing and catching.

On offense, we decided to throw a little more because we thought that would be more effective against their scheme. David told me during the week he thought Tee was ready to have a breakout game. We still wanted to be the more physical team and run the football, but if South Carolina loaded up to stop the run, we were going to attack with Tee throwing the ball.

When you're playing on the road, you always want to practice on the same field you are playing on the next day. The reason for this is to give your players some familiarity with not only the field but the stadium as well. The practice the day before the game is called a "walk-through." It's so named because the players go over their plays and sets in shorts, and not at full speed.

During our walk-through, I again reminded our players of the danger in not playing at our highest level the next day. The funny thing is, I didn't sense we weren't focused or didn't feel like our team wasn't going to be at its best. I guess if you've ever been upset, you never quit coaching that way when playing teams that you are supposed to beat.

Our team played at a very high level against South Carolina. Our offensive team had its most productive game of the season by far in terms of execution. Tee Martin was literally on fire. He broke all kinds of records by completing twenty-three consecutive passes. Obviously, our receivers played extremely well for Tee to throw that many completions in a row. I do not know if I have ever seen a college game with a passing effort more impressive than ours was for most of this game. Tee set an NCAA record with his twenty-third consecutive completion.

Defensively, we stopped South Carolina's running game and forced them to throw the football. We defended them extremely well throughout the critical part of this game and stayed in control of the game almost from the start. It was an outstanding team effort.

South Carolina scored a couple of touchdowns on our second- and third-team defenses. This points to some problems in today's world of the B.C.S.: 1) I expect the guys that are on the field to get them stopped; 2) You have to decide who you are going to be fair to: the second- or third-team players that deserve to play or the top players that held them; 3) Do you risk injury to starters to please a computer somewhere in Seattle or disappoint the fans when the opposition scores a couple of late touchdowns and the computer lowers your ranking? These kinds of issues make it tough on a coach.

In the locker room after the game, I told our players that I had challenged them not to look past South Carolina and to play at their highest level, and they responded like champions. I let Tee know how proud I was of not only him, but also our receivers and offensive line that helped him complete all those throws in a row. I told our team that they had been practicing and playing like champions and not to forget how they got to be 7-0—by taking it one game at a time.

We sang our Tennessee Victory Song and celebrated as the guys were thrilled for Tee. Our team had rallied around Tee Martin. They respected him for being patient and working hard, for his skill and poise under pressure. They admired him for his attitude toward life, toward people, toward school and football. They closed ranks around him when he wasn't throwing the ball particularly well earlier in the year. After the South Carolina game, they rejoiced with their quarterback in whom they had always believed on his record-setting day. And so did I—we had climbed one more rung on the ladder.

> **I had challenged them not to look past South Carolina and to play at their highest level, and they responded like champions.**

CHAPTER • 11

Alabama-Birmingham

We were now ranked number two in the nation behind Ohio State and gaining ground. The Bowl Championship race was now in the newspaper nearly every day and we appeared to be in a favorable position to play in the Fiesta Bowl, which would be the site of this season's national-championship game. Our team and staff returned home and faced a lot more questions about the B.C.S., the computers and our schedule, and Arkansas than they did about our next opponent—UAB. Obviously, this was of some concern to me.

I told our team in the team meeting early in the week that they had convinced me they had the leadership and maturity to not look past any opponent. My concern was not in overlooking a team but in being distracted by things over which we had no control. That's what I shared with our players. I said we have little control over how some computer ranks us or how the Bowl Championship people rank us. But we do have ultimate control over our games against UAB, Arkansas, Kentucky, and Vanderbilt. I told them that there was only one thing that I was sure of—that was if we gave our best effort in these last five games we would play for the national championship.

Our next hurdle was the University of Alabama-Birmingham. UAB was a relative newcomer to Division I football. They were coached by Watson Brown, who for many years had coached in our conference. Watson has always been known for his offensive mind, and I thought his playing against us so much over the years would benefit his team in this game.

I knew Watson would do a good job with the personnel he had. Watching them on film certainly bore that out. UAB ran a lot, was multiple on defense, ran a lot of option on offense, and had the players to do it effectively. By running the ball, it gave UAB a chance to shorten the football game, which is a major advantage if you're facing a team with more talent than you.

```
ALA. BIRMINGHAM              OFFENSIVE PRACTICE SCHEDULE
WORKOUT: #51           DATE: TUESDAY, NOVEMBER 3, 1998
GEAR:                  TIME: 2:30 MEET; 3:55 FLEX
PLACE: U.HUDSON        WINNING EDGE: FUNDAMENTALS
```

PER / TIME	C-G	T	TE'S	WR	QB	RB
1 / 3:55	FLEX --->					
2 / 4:02	FIELD GOAL --------------------------->		WARM UP	AGILITIES WARM UP QUICK THROWS	FG
3 / 4:05	FISHHOOK S & S REACH	COMBOS P SLIP	PUNT &	PUNT RETURN	CROSSING ROUTES BUCKET THROWS	PUNT RETURN
4 / 4:17	GUARD PULLS	POP & TURN GAP G-PULL CTR/SWEEP	POP & TURN W/OT'S SLED	BALL DRILL ROUTE WORK	T/A -------->	
5 / 4:25	MIDDLE DRILL ------------------------>			RVA ---------->		MIDDLE DRILL
6 / 4:33	PERIMETER --->					
7 / 4:43	BPU ------------------------------->			1 ON 1 --------> VS DB'S		BPU
8 / 4:51	PASS SETS ----------> & DRAW VS RIP & TWISTS		OUTSIDE VS UAB ------------------------->			
9 / 4:59	TEAM - RUN - MIX -->					
10 / 5:09	TEAM - P.A. & QUICK GAMES -------------------------------------->					
11 / 5:19	LOVERS LANE ---------->		OUTSIDE VS DEFENSE --------------------->			
12 / 5:27	TEAM - RUN - MIX -->					
13 / 5:37	TEAM VS DEFENSE --->					
14 / 5:45	CONDITIONING / KOC					

**UAB Week Practice Schedules
(text resumes on page 112)**

DEFENSIVE PRACTICE SCHEDULE

WORKOUT: TUE-UAB DATE: 11-3-98
GEAR: FULL TIME: 2:30 MEET 3:55 FLEX
PLACE: U HUDSON WINNING EDGE: **PHYSICAL PLAY**

EMPHASIS
FAV. RUNS/PA PASS

#	Time	TACKLES	ENDS	LB'ERS	SECONDARY
1	3:55		TEAM	FLEX	
2	4:02		PAT	/ FG BLOCK	
3	4:05	GET OFF(CHUTES) / MVMTS (CHUTE)	PUNT / PUNT	PRO/COVER / BLK/RET	
4	4:17	BLK REACT / RCH (TACKLE) / DWN	WINNING DLB TEAM 41 QB CALL	EDGE W DRILL MEDICINE BALL LOAD BLOCK	FOOTWORK / KEY READS / W/ TACKLING
5	4:25	½ LINE OPTION	KEY ————————→		↓
6	4:33	TEAM BLITZ	VS. UAB ————————→		
7	4:43	FRONT 7			1 ON 1 VS. WRs
8	4:51	BLOCK REACT / TRAP / INF / FOLD ON LB	5 TECH / TRAP / COUNTER	OUTSIDE	VS. UAB
9	4:59	TEAM	VS. UAB ————————→		
10	5:09	TEAM	VS. UAB ————————→		
11	5:19	PASS RUSH	VS. OFF. LINE	O/S	VS. OFFENSE
12	5:27	TEAM	VS. UAB ————————→		
13	5:37	TEAM	VS. OFFENSE ————————→		
14	5:45	CONDITIONING	/ KICKOFF COV.		
15		88			

ALABAMA-BIRMINGHAM

```
ALA.BIRMINGHAM           OFFENSIVE PRACTICE SCHEDULE
WORKOUT: #53             DATE: THURSDAY, NOVEMBER 5, 1998
GEAR:    SHORTS          TIME: 2:30 MEET;3:40 FULMER;4:05 FLEX
PLACE:   U.HUDSON        WINNING EDGE: DRESS REHEARSAL
```

PER TIME	C-G	T	TE'S	WR	QB	RB
1 / 4:05	FLEX --->					
2 / 4:12	KOC					
3	KOR					
4	PUNT					
5	PUNT RETURN					
6 / 4:47	TEAM - G.L. - 2 POINT PLAYS ----------------------------->					
7 / 4:57	TEAM - BACKED UP - STALL - SHORT YARDAGE ---------------->					
8 / 5:07	TEAM - ORANGE AREA - 3RD DOWNS -------------------------->					
9 / 5:17	TEAM - PERIMETER - MIX ---------------------------------->					
10 / 5:27	TEAM - TAKE OFF --------------------------------------->					
11 / 5:37	2 MINUTE VS DEFENSE					
12 / 5:47	88					
13						
14						

DEFENSIVE PRACTICE SCHEDULE

WORKOUT: THUR-UAB **DATE:** 11-05-98 **EMPHASIS**
GEAR: SHORTS **TIME:** 2:30 MTG, 4:05 FLEX ALL PHASES
PLACE: HUDSON **WINNING EDGE:** GAME PREPARATION

#	Time	TACKLES	ENDS	LB'ERS	SECONDARY
1	4:05	TEAM	FLEX		
2	4:12	4I TECH / 3 TECH/STAB	KICK	OFF COVERAGE	
3		MVMTS COLEMAN!	KICK	OFF RETURN	
4		PITCH ENDS SPRINTOUT X/TWIST	PUNT	PRO/COVER	
5		PUNT	BLOCK	RET	SAFE
6	4:47	TEAM	VS. UAB		
7	4:57	TEAM	VS. UAB		
8	5:07	TEAM	VS. UAB		
9	5:17	TEAM	VS. UAB		
10	5:27	TEAM	VS. UAB		
11	5:37	TEAM	VS. OFFENSE		2 MINUTE
12	5:47	88			
13					
14					
15					

ALABAMA-BIRMINGHAM   111

Watching UAB on defense, the first thing I noticed was the quickness of their front seven. They had some linemen who could really move, especially Pernell Davis. Their defense reminded me some of Syracuse, a little undersized but with lots of quickness and movement.

During the week, Coach Brown evidently made some comments about how his team had no chance to win, but he expected his young players would fight. Those comments were read by some of our players, and I warned our team he was trying to set us up. In fact, I told our team that if we didn't plan as well as we could and play at our highest level, UAB could beat us or play us very close.

After Friday's light practice, I told our guys that they had prepared well through practice this week, and I believed they were physically and mentally ready to play. I talked for a minute about focus and pointed out that some people are easily gratified, but champions are never satisfied. I wanted our team to stay hungry.

Homecoming day was beautiful. I told our guys in the locker room to play with great passion and to have fun. If we played with the same physical and aggressive manner that we had all season, we would be just fine. Our group had a hungry look in their eyes when they left the locker room.

UAB gave us a hard-fought game, although we managed to stay focused and win, 37-13. Defensively, they were better than I thought, and they made some yardage running the ball against us. Overall, we were the more physical team and the more talented team, and we won fairly convincingly. It wasn't our best game, but UAB deserves some credit for that.

Our team had just gotten into the dressing room after the game when word broke that number-one-ranked Ohio State had been upset by Michigan State. The locker room erupted in cheers. We sang our Tennessee Victory Song with a little more enthusiasm today. The players were excited about the possibility of being ranked number one in the nation. I've got to admit as I drove home Saturday night, I was excited, too. It had been a great Homecoming day at Tennessee. We had climbed another step.

Will Overstreet moves in on Georgia's Quincy Carter thinking "sack". (UNIVERSITY OF TENNESSEE)

Working the kinks out before we meet Alabama. (TOM RAYMOND)

Not a cloud in the sky for the Alabama game. (TOM RAYMOND)

When Tee decides to take off and run, watch out! (Tom Raymond)

Good sportsmanship need not be ignored in the heat of battle. (Tom Raymond)

Travis Henry needs to watch out, too, as he tries to keep his head in the game against an Alabama defender. (Tom Raymond)

I'm sure in this instance I was shouting words of encouragement. (TOM RAYMOND)

Defensive end DeAngelo Lloyd tries to strip the ball as he's coached to do. (Tom Raymond)

We're from Tennessee and proud of it. (Tom Raymond)

Against Alabama we are always careful to dot our i's and cross our t's. (Tom Raymond)

Defensive back Dwayne Goodrich fires 'em up! (TOM RAYMOND)

Wide receiver Cedrick Wilson has Alabama company in going for a pass. (TOM RAYMOND)

Preparing to lead the troops onto the field at South Carolina. (STEVE WOLTMANN PHOTO)

Tee was nearly perfect against South Carolina. (UNIVERSITY OF TENNESSEE)

Travis Henry busts a move against South Carolina. (STEVE WOLTMANN PHOTO)

Wide receiver Eric Parker gains some yards of his own. (STEVE WOLTMANN PHOTO)

Defensive end DeAngelo Lloyd gives chase! (STEVE WOLTMANN PHOTO)

Wide receiver Jeremaine Copeland showing some of the moves that helped him score a touchdown against South Carolina. (STEVE WOLTMANN PHOTO)

Running back Travis Stephens lowering his head in anticipation of contact. (STEVE WOLTMANN PHOTO)

The Tennessee spirit is alive and well as the cheerleaders lead us onto the field for the Alabama-Birmingham game.
(TOM RAYMOND)

Al Wilson calls defensive signals against Alabama-Birmingham. (TOM RAYMOND)

Linebacker Eric Westmoreland drags a UAB player down from behind. (TOM RAYMOND)

Cedrick Wilson about to hit full stride with another reception in hand. (TOM RAYMOND)

Jeff Hall's classic body posture with left arm raised and fist clenched shows a placekicker's determination. (TOM RAYMOND)

Tackle Chad Clifton appears to be a one-man line blocking for placekicker Jeff Hall. (UNIVERSITY OF TENNESSEE)

Okay, so these photos weren't taken at the same time, but when else will you see me and Al Wilson with both of our mouths closed at the same time? (TOM RAYMOND)

Travis Henry picking a hole against UAB. (TOM RAYMOND)

The Vol Navy has arrived for the Arkansas game. (Tim Clark photo)

Tee Martin, up close, as he calls signals. (University of Tennessee)

Peerless Price looking for another big gain, this time against Arkansas.
(TOM RAYMOND)

Wide receiver Jeremaine Copeland had something to say here.
(TOM RAYMOND)

Our front line was poised for anything in '98. (TOM RAYMOND)

Our band struts its stuff for Vol fans. (TIM CLARK PHOTO)

Linebacker Al Wilson made a lot of great tackles in 1998. (TOM RAYMOND)

Travis Henry wards off a would-be Arkansas tackler with a textbook stiff-arm. (TOM RAYMOND)

Outgoing UT President Dr. Joe Johnson and his wife, Pat, get a much-deserved welcome before our game with Kentucky. (TOM RAYMOND)

The Vol Walk has become a great Tennessee football tradition. (TIM CLARK PHOTO)

Tennessee ballcarriers never go down without a fight. (TOM RAYMOND)

Shawn Bryson breaking a long run against Kentucky. (TOM RAYMOND)

Raynoch Thompson puts the squeeze on Kentucky's superlative quarterback, Tim Couch. (TOM RAYMOND)

Orange is the obvious color of choice even for our youngest fans.
(TIM CLARK PHOTO)

Halftimes at UT games are always special.
(TOM RAYMOND)

Defensive back Steve Johnson breaks up a Kentucky pass. (TOM RAYMOND)

Vicky, my wife, is a real sport about everything that goes with being the UT head coach's wife. (University of Tennessee)

Tee Martin is always at home in or near the end zone. (Tom Raymond)

Tight end John Finlayson is as intense on the sideline as he is on the field. (TOM RAYMOND)

Shaun Ellis made a remarkable recovery from a terrible automobile accident. (TOM RAYMOND)

Raynoch Thompson puts another good lick on Kentucky's Tim Couch. (TOM RAYMOND)

Linebacker Judd Granzow makes some nice contact. (Tom Raymond)

CHAPTER • 12

Arkansas

The Sunday after Homecoming was an exciting day around our football complex, and probably around our entire state as well. The anticipation of being ranked number one, coupled with the anticipation of playing a crucial game next Saturday, created a great atmosphere for Tennessee football fans.

I didn't have to wonder very long about how it felt to be ranked at the top as on Monday the Tennessee Volunteers were ranked number one in the polls. We were 8-0 and ready to play undefeated Arkansas, a game the media had hyped for several weeks.

What did it feel like to be ranked number one? I've got to be honest and say I felt first and foremost a lot of pride. I also felt a lot of responsibility, as if it had been so long since we were at the top. I wanted to keep us there as long as possible. There was also a sense of satisfaction, but I didn't dwell on that for very long. I knew that was the easiest way to have a short stay at the top. The bottom line is I didn't spend a lot of time thinking about this—I had my hands full worrying about Arkansas.

We met Monday after the UAB game, and I congratulated our players on the victory. I then told them if there was ever a girl they wanted to ask out on a date and were a little scared to ask, that while they were ranked number one was the time to do it. Our guys loved that. I was just trying to have some fun with them, and it really broke any tension they had.

I spent most of my time in this meeting talking about staying focused on our mission. Our mission hadn't changed since last winter—and that was to be more physical, run the football, and stop the run. We weren't

ARKANSAS   **OFFENSIVE PRACTICE SCHEDULE**
WORKOUT: #55   DATE: TUESDAY, NOVEMBER 10, 1998
GEAR: FULL   TIME: 2:30 MEET; 3:55 FLEX
PLACE: U.HUDSON WINNING EDGE: BALL SECURITY

PER TIME	C-G	T	TE'S	WR	QB	RB
1 3:55	FLEX --->					
2 4:02	FG ------------------------------>			WARM UP	AGILITIES DROPS WARM UP	FG
3 4:05	S/S REACH	POP/TURN STEPS	PUNT ---------> & P.R.		QK. THROWS CROSSING ROUTES CORNERS	PUNT & P.R.
4 4:15	CTR/G RUBS *COP 8/9	ZEBRA VS 7 "VS STORM	TECH'S LOOKS	ROUTE WORK CROSSING ROUTES	T/A --------->	
5 4:23	MIDDLE ---------------------------------> DRILL			RVA ---------->		MIDDLE DRILL
6 4:31	PERIMETER -->					
7 4:39	BPU ------------------------------>			1 ON 1 ---------> VS DB'S		BPU
8 4:47	PASS PRO VS MAD DOG		OUTSIDE VS ARKANSAS ------------------>			
9 4:55	TEAM --->					
10 5:05	TEAM --->					
11 5:15	LOVERS ----------> LANE		OUTSIDE VS DEFENSE ----------------->			
12 5:22	TEAM --->					
13 5:32	TEAM VS DEFENSE --->					
14 5:40	CONDITIONING	& KOC	5:50 88			

Arkansas Week Practice Schedules
(text resumes on page 118)

114   A PERFECT SEASON

DEFENSIVE PRACTICE SCHEDULE

WORKOUT: TUE-ARK
GEAR: FULL
PLACE: U HUDSON
DATE: 11-10-98
TIME: 2:30 MEET 3:55 FLEX
WINNING EDGE: DO MY JOB

EMPHASIS
FAV. RUNS/PA PASS

#	Time	TACKLES	ENDS	LB'ERS	SECONDARY
1	3:55		TEAM FLEX		
2	4:02		PAT / FG BLOCK		
3	4:05	GET OFF (CHUTES) MVMTS (UPFIELD)	PUNT / PUNT	PRO/COVER BLK/RET	
4	4:15	HANDS EXPLOSION GET OFF BLOCKER TO TACKLE	SLED WORK 1. CHEAT VS PWO 2. 6 TECH RUB	TAKE ON DRILL WAGGLE KEY	FOOTWORK HANDS DRILL ---- SLANTS FADES
5	4:23	FRONT 7 BLITZ	VS RUN →		COVER 8 TACKLING ---- FORMATION ADJ.
6	4:31	TEAM BLITZ	VS. ARK →		→
7	4:39	FRONT 7	VS ARKANSAS		1 ON 1 VS. WRs
8	4:47	PLAY ACTION PASS/HANDS QB PUMP	PLAY ACTION PASS RUSH TOSS THROWBACK	O/SUS	ARKANSAS
9	4:55	TEAM	VS. ARK →		→
10	5:05	TEAM	VS. ARK		→
11	5:15	PASS RUSH	VS. OFF. LINE	O/S	VS. OFFENSE
12	5:22	TEAM	VS. ARK →		→
13	5:32	TEAM	VS. OFFENSE →		→
14	5:40	CONDITIONING	5:50 88		

ARKANSAS   115

```
ARKANSAS                    OFFENSIVE PRACTICE SCHEDULE
WORKOUT: #57      DATE: THURSDAY, NOVEMBER 12, 1998
GEAR:    SHORTS   TIME: 2:00 MEET;3:40 FULMER;4:05 FLEX
PLACE:   U.HUDSON WINNING EDGE: DRESS REHEARSAL
```

PER TIME	C-G	T	TE'S	WR	QB	RB
1 4:05	FLEX ——→					
2 4:12	KOC					
3	KOR					
4	PUNT					
5	PUNT RETURN					
6 4:47	TEAM - G.L. - 2 POINT PLAYS ————————————————→					
7 4:57	TEAM - BACKE UP - STALL - SHORT YARDAGE ——————→					
8 5:07	TEAM - ORANGE AREA - 3RD DOWNS ————————————————→					
9 5:17	TEAM - PERIMETER - MIX ————————————————————————→					
10 5:27	TEAM - TAKE OFF ———————————————————————————————→					
11 5:37	2 MINUTE VS DEFENSE					
12 5:47	88					
13						
14						

A PERFECT SEASON

DEFENSIVE PRACTICE SCHEDULE

EMPHASIS

WORKOUT: THUR-ARK DATE: 11-12-98 ALL PHASES
GEAR: SHORTS TIME: 2:30 MTG, 4:05 FLEX
PLACE: HUDSON WINNING EDGE: GAME PREPARATION

#	TACKLES	ENDS	LB'ERS	SECONDARY
1 4:05	TEAM	FLEX		
2 4:12	DROP HOOK RUN 1ST	KICK	OFF COVERAGE	
3	STAR 2 INTO BDY	KICK	OFF RETURN	
4	TWIST VS RUN	PUNT	PRO/COVER	
5	PUNT	BLOCK	RET	SAFE
6 4:47	TEAM	VS. ARKANSAS	BACKED UP	
7 4:57	TEAM	VS. ARKANSAS	OPEN FIELD	
8 5:07	TEAM	VS. ARKANSAS	OPEN FIELD	
9 5:17	TEAM	VS. ARKANSAS	OPEN FIELD TO ORANGE AREA	
10 5:27	TEAM	VS. ARKANSAS	ORANGE AREA TO GOALLINE	
11 5:37	TEAM	VS. OFFENSE		2 MINUTE
12 5:47	88			
13				
14				

going to change that whether we were playing Arkansas, Kentucky, or Vanderbilt. I further told our guys not to tense up by thinking of these games as do or die. I ended this meeting by asking our guys if they thought we would practice differently, use different schemes, or change our philosophy because we were now ranked number one. I answered my own question by telling them that we got to be the top-ranked team in America by being fundamentally prepared and laying it on the line for sixty minutes—and that was how we were going to stay on top.

After I looked at Arkansas on tape, I could see why they were undefeated. They were strong, physical, and athletic on both sides of the line of scrimmage. Our offensive staff was extremely impressed with their defense. Danny Ford, their last head coach, had left some good players behind who had played a lot of snaps in our league, and first-year Arkansas head coach Houston Nutt and his staff had done a great job of coaching these guys and creating enthusiasm in their program.

Defensively, the strength of their football team was their defensive front. Arkansas had thick and quick guys, like Ryan Hale, Melvin Bradley, and C. J. McClain. These guys were all quality defensive front people, and they were all veteran players. Being so strong up front made it difficult for teams to run on Arkansas. Their scheme was also designed to stop the run, because they always had one more guy in the front than you had blockers for.

Their linebackers were aggressive and fast. They had moved one of their secondary players, Zac Painter, basically to linebacker and were sacrificing a little size in their linebackers to get more speed. Arkansas's secondary played a lot of man-to-man coverage and had very good players back there. I was especially impressed with one of their safeties, Kenoy Kennedy.

Arkansas's defense was all based on pressure. They would often line up seven or eight defenders at the line of scrimmage. And they blitzed early and often. In the games that I watched on film, their blitzes would often put opposing offenses in terrible down-and-distance situations. That was the benefit of taking the risk with so much pressure, while the risk is in giving up large chunks of yardage at a time.

Our game plan to attack this defense was simply to run the football right at them. We knew that with so many defenders near the line of scrimmage and their willingness to shoot the gaps so much, we could run some plays into the strength of their pressure. But we wanted to keep pounding it at them, because I believed if we did that two things would eventually happen. One, our size would wear them down late in the ball game. And, two, our play-action opportunities would be there throughout the game. The key for us was to keep pounding and hold onto the football. I felt if we protected the ball well, we would eventually have a lot of success running the football against Arkansas.

In watching Arkansas on film offensively, I could see the complete package of players that made them a very potent offense. Any good offense starts with a strong offensive line. Arkansas had probably the best one I had seen all year. They had four seniors in that group, and all of them had played a lot of football. Their right guard, Brandon Burlsworth, was outstanding. As a group, they could pass- and run-block, which made them that much more effective. Their tight end, Joe Dean Davenport, was a big, tall player who caught the ball well, and they used him effectively.

Perhaps the biggest improvement and reason for Arkansas's tremendous turnaround was the play of quarterback Clint Stoerner. Stoerner was an accurate passer who made good decisions and a guy who appeared to be a fine leader of his team. He certainly had some talented receivers to throw the ball to. Anthony Lucas was one of the better receivers in the country, and Emanuel Smith and Michael Williams joined him to form an exceptional group.

Arkansas had two fine tailbacks who both ran hard. They were not afraid to pound it at you offensively because of the strength of their offensive line and the ability of the two backs, Madre Hill and Chrys Chukwuma. Defenses could not bunch up too much or Stoerner would flip it outside to Lucas and his group. You see what I mean when I said earlier they had a complete package for their offense. When you combine skill with the fact they were playing with confidence, it is easy to understand how they had won so many games so decisively.

John and his defensive staff had watched a lot of Arkansas. They were convinced, and so was I, that we had to stop their running game. We couldn't let their offensive line dominate the game. We also had to stop the big play, like the throw over the top, to be successful. I felt like we had to really get after their quarterback, as well. Stoerner was making big plays, but if you had to pick your poison, we were going to stop the run and try to pressure him into making difficult throws.

We had a strong week of practice. I told our staff early in the week that if we wanted to play aggressively Saturday, then we had to coach aggressively during the week. I let our defensive coaches know that I thought it important to play a lot of front people, something we had worked on all year long. Our staff did a good job throughout the week in setting up the best scout team they could to simulate Arkansas. That's a little thing—but all those little things add up to success.

We practiced the wet-ball drill a lot on Wednesday. Our trainer, Mike Rollo, was in charge of getting the weather forecast and the long-range forecast for Saturday was rain. Our practice pace was good and our guys were really anxious to play Arkansas.

I told our team after we finished practice Thursday that Arkansas was a really fine team that presented us with a great challenge. I let them know that all year people had been predicting that they would fail in this game or that game, but none of those people were on our team. They didn't know our character, our heart, or our fight. Those things, more than talent or home field or our number-one ranking, gave us the winning edge.

It had been a long time since two undefeated Southeastern Conference teams had played each other in mid-November. I told our guys in the locker room before kickoff that it was this kind of game that they came to Tennessee to play in. Al Wilson told his teammates that we had come too far, too long, for anybody to mess our season up and he wasn't going to stand for it. His emotion, and that of the other leaders on this team, reverberated throughout our team.

It was a great college football game. Arkansas came out strong and played an exceptional first half and led at half-time. Uncharacteristically, we turned the football over several times. In the second half, we got into a better flow, and late in the fourth quarter it was a very close game. We were fortunate to recover a fumble around midfield with little over a minute to go. Our offensive line and running game took over, and in five consecutive running plays we scored a touchdown to win the game, 28-24. It was truly a

We practiced the wet-ball drill a lot on Wednesday... The long-range forecast for Saturday was rain.

great finish for the Volunteers and a heartbreaker, I know, for Arkansas, which played an outstanding game.

In the locker room my emotions were nearly spent, and I know our players' were as well. I told our guys how proud I was of them for battling and battling through this game. It had been one of those games as a coach that you look at and say, "My team really has been listening." We coaches preach to never quit, to never give up no matter the circumstances. Boy, when your team doesn't quit and keeps fighting even when the odds are against you—I can't tell you how proud it makes you feel.

It took a tremendous amount of courage to run the ball with less than two minutes left. I credit David Cutcliffe, the offensive staff, and players for their effort in that drive. The offensive line dominated the line of scrimmage. Travis Henry ran like a bull, shedding tacklers and falling forward. Our wide receivers, especially Jeremaine Copeland, had several great downfield blocks to allow us to get those extra yards. The entire drive was a testament of will to win.

The last thing I told our guys before we sang our Tennessee Victory Song was that every championship team wins a game late like this. The reason is because championship teams have character, heart, and leadership, and they never quit until the sixty minutes have elapsed. What a game! We made a big step up the ladder.

CHAPTER • 13

Kentucky

One surefire way for a coach to lose the feeling of elation after winning a big game is to turn on the tape of your next opponent. Your emotion of elation quickly turns into a whole new set of worries, particularly if your next opponent is a border rival and, more particularly, if they've got Tim Couch at quarterback, a group of talented wide receivers, and a veteran offensive line.

I couldn't have been more pleased with the gutty effort our players had made in our victory over Arkansas. I wasn't very pleased with our execution in the game at times, but I was proud of the character we showed. That was our fourth win this season over an unbeaten team. We stayed ranked number one in the country. All of this was of little solace to me as I sat alone Sunday in the back of my office and watched Tim Couch throw the ball up and down the field against some of the best teams in our league.

We had several of our defensive guys show up Sunday at the football complex to get a jump on studying Kentucky. A lot of that group was either on the field or watching the year before as Kentucky piled all those yards on us. I wasn't the least bit surprised at the number of players who engaged in film study on their own. That's the mark of a mature team that not only has the will to win, but the will to prepare to win, as I like to tell our players.

As you could imagine, with our ranking and our having just won a dramatic game over an undefeated team, our whole campus was ripe with enthusiasm. But our football players continued to take a very businesslike approach to our meetings and our practices. I had commented to the staff about that several times earlier in the year, but I really saw that trait as kind of a trademark of our team. They were certainly excited and thrilled over that last victory, but by the next day they were already focused on the

DEFENSIVE PRACTICE SCHEDULE

WORKOUT: TUE-KY DATE: 11-17-98 **EMPHASIS**
GEAR: FULL TIME: 2:30 MEET 3:55 FLEX FAV. RUNS/PA PASS
PLACE: U HUDSON WINNING EDGE: PRESSURE

#	Time	TACKLES	ENDS	LB'ERS	SECONDARY
1	3:55	TEAM	FLEX		
2	4:02	PAT	/ FG BLOCK		
3	4:05	GET OFF(CHUTES) MVMTS (CAT)	PUNT	PRO/COVER	
4	4:10	HANDS EXPLOSION GET OFF BLOCKER TO TACKLE	(WINNING EDGE) CUT CALL W DRILL BACK AWAY DRAW S/F TECH TECH TOSS		SQUAT TECH MOTION PACE
5	4:18	SLIDE G (DEAL) AIM TANGO ACE/TRICK	DRAW SET	ZONE DROPS	3 RATT 1 PIRATE
6	4:26	TEAM	VS. KENTUCKY →		
7	4:36	PUNT	SAFE	RET	
8	4:41	FRONT 7	VS. KENTUCKY		1 ON 1 VS. WR'S
9	4:49	PASS RUSH FL. CTR SPIN & CTR	PASS RUSH	O/S VS.	KENTUCKY
10	4:57	TEAM	VS. KY		
11	5:07	TEAM	VS. KY		
12	5:17	PASS RUSH	VS. OFF. LINE	O/S	VS. OFFENSE
13	5:27	TEAM	VS. KY		
14	5:37	TEAM	VS. OFFENSE		
15	5:47	KICKOFF COV	/ CONDITIONING	55/16	88

Kentucky Week Practice Schedules (text resumes on page 126)

DEFENSIVE PRACTICE SCHEDULE   **EMPHASIS**

WORKOUT: THUR-KY   DATE: 11-19-98   ALL PHASES
GEAR: SHORTS   TIME: 2:30 MTG, 4:05 FLEX
PLACE: HUDSON   WINNING EDGE: GAME PREPARATION

#	TACKLES	ENDS	LB'ERS	SECONDARY
1 4:05	TEAM	FLEX		
2 4:12	DOG CAT GO	KICK	OFF COVERAGE	
3	DRAW CALL BEAR	KICK	OFF RETURN	
4		PUNT	PRO / COVER	
5	PUNT	BLOCK	RET	SAFE
6 4:47	TEAM	VS. KENTUCKY		BACKED UP
7 4:57	TEAM	VS. KENTUCKY		OPEN FIELD
8 5:07	TEAM	VS. KENTUCKY		OPEN FIELD
9 5:17	TEAM	VS. KENTUCKY		OPEN FIELD TO ORANGE AREA
10 5:25	TEAM	VS. KENTUCKY		ORANGE AREA TO GOALLINE
11 5:33	TEAM	VS. OFFENSE		2 MINUTE
12	88			
13				
14				
15				

KENTUCKY   125

upcoming opponent. I really think this is one of the things that made this team special, and special to coach.

Tim Couch, as I mentioned earlier, was a very gifted quarterback whom we had tried very hard to sign. He was a player a lot like Peyton Manning in that he had both an outstanding arm and a feel for the passing game. Couch had breathed new life into Kentucky's program, and our game was the game of the year for them. Their offense had had a lot of success against us in the previous year.

> [Tim] Couch had breathed new life into Kentucky's program, and our game was the game of the year for them.

In reviewing Kentucky on film, it's clear you had to do three things to be successful against their offense. One, you must pressure the quarterback and get to him. Two, you must limit their production in the running game, which means you must stop their draw play. And, three, you must tackle well—especially their backs and receivers in their short passing game. We didn't do a good job last year in the latter two categories.

Kentucky was very dangerous offensively. While Couch might have been the best quarterback in the country, they had lots of other talent offensively. Their offensive line was made up, kind of like Arkansas, mostly of seniors, and they did a really good job. They did an especially good job in pass protection. They had several talented receivers, with Craig Yeast being one of the fastest and most dangerous players in our league. Their running backs, Anthony White and Derrick Homer, were both good players who could run and catch the ball well. I really thought Homer and Yeast were two guys we had to pay special attention to in this game.

To stop Kentucky, we had to do what I said we didn't do well the year before. Their offense was built around the short passing game. They would throw underneath the coverage if you played soft, and they would throw over your head if the protection held. Our defense had to apply more pressure and tackle better in the open field. I told our defensive guys in practice that we needed a ferocious rush Saturday. The line to remember Saturday, I said, was "Pressure and then more pressure." I felt we could get pressure with our front people, especially as the game wore on.

Defensively, we spent a lot of practice time working on our tackling fundamentals and our nickel-and-dime package. This package puts five or six defensive backs on the field with your best pass rushers. I wrote on the board in our locker room "Stay Hungry" earlier in the week, and I think our guys did exactly that on the practice field all week.

Kentucky's defense was as big a gambling defense as you'll ever see. Obviously, they would take chances in order to get the ball back to their offense as quickly as possible. I thought their two tackles, Marvin Major and Mark Jacobs, were good players and gave them some push inside. Kentucky gives you a lot of different looks defensively. The one constant, however, is to expect some sort of blitz on run or pass plays from somewhere. Their safety, Jeff Zurcher, showed up all over the place on film and I thought he and one of their linebackers, Jeff Snedegar, were really sound tacklers.

Our offensive staff worked hard all week in meetings and practices with Tee and the offense on reading and reacting to Kentucky's alignments. They thought we had a chance for several big plays in this game if we recognized and reacted well. Mike Barry and Mark Bradley worked our offensive line hard on picking up their run stunts and blitzes. The entire staff did a good job in preparing our guys for this game. It showed Saturday.

From the first time I talked to our players until we left the locker room to play the game Saturday, I harped on watching out for the trick plays. Kentucky called a very high number of fake punts and kicks, onside kicks, reverses…you name it. Those kind of calls can be momentum swingers—either way. We put special emphasis on executing our assignments on special teams and reminded our players to always expect the unexpected.

I felt like we had prepared like champions all week for this game. I told our players late in the week we had a chance to pounce on Kentucky early and take the fight out of them. To do that, we had to be aggressive on both sides of the ball. And not just in our play, I told everybody, but in our *play calling*. I let them know that we were prepared for whatever trick plays they might run, and we needed to make them backfire on Kentucky every time they tried one. Be physical and be aware—that was the winning edge against Kentucky.

This had been a difficult week for Kentucky, as they were going through an emotional trauma resulting from a terrible tragedy. They had lost two young men and had another severely injured in a car accident earlier in the week. As with your own children, you worry about this, and it was complicated by the fact that alcohol was involved. This was very sad for the Kentucky program and the Kentucky people, and we said a prayer for them. It also gave me a podium to talk about the responsibilities they have when they get behind a wheel or in a car with someone whose judgment and reactions are impaired by drugs or alcohol. I know the players get tired of me harping on this sort of thing, but I do anyway. One young life saved is worth the effort.

We constantly talk to our players about the pitfalls that are out there. Drugs and alcohol, agents, gambling, and unscrupulous boosters. We also talk to them about treating women with respect, having academic integrity, and so forth.

Again—our guys had been good listeners.

This game was an emotional one. It was the last home game at Neyland Stadium for our seniors. When we gathered in the locker room right before the game, the senior leadership and their will not to lose was obvious to anyone. Several of them said emotional words, with the common bond being they were not going to lose for the first time this year in their last home game. **Our guys weren't tense or nervous as we headed into the tunnel—they were anxious to get on the field.**

It was a great Saturday for Tennessee fans. We jumped on Kentucky early and soundly defeated them, 59-21. Our team played just like it had practiced—hard, aware, and with a purpose. It was a great team victory for us and a wonderful setting for the final game for our seniors.

The locker room was a fun place. It was a beautiful day as our players played well and everybody got to play. While we were all happy with our performance and the victory, I noticed a few sad eyes for a moment as we sang our Tennessee Victory Song. Some of the seniors realized they had just taken their orange jerseys off for the last time in a Tennessee locker room. I told our players that this was one of those rare times when you could feel both happy and sad at the same time. I said I thought there would be only one feeling better than running through the *T*, and that would be walking off the field in Arizona knowing that you were national champions. That struck a chord. We climbed one more rung that day.

Defensive end Will Overstreet tries to ward off a Vandy blocker. (TIM CLARK PHOTO)

Darwin Walker and Eric Westmoreland helped make the going tough for Vanderbilt. (UNIVERSITY OF TENNESSEE)

Jamal Lewis in street clothes, wishing, as we did, that he could have been suited up for the late-season stretch run. (TOM RAYMOND)

Defensive end Roger Alexander makes a big hit against Mississippi State in the SEC Championship Game. (TOM RAYMOND)

Travis Stephens dives for more yardage. (TOM RAYMOND)

I hear that! (UNIVERSITY OF TENNESSEE)

Athletic director Doug Dickey shares a victory moment with linebacker Al Wilson. (TOM RAYMOND)

Being all wet is A-OK when it's after winning the SEC Championship. (TOM RAYMOND)

Corey Terry is proud to be a Vol, too! (Tom Raymond)

When he wasn't directing our offense, Tee was doing a nice job guest-conducting the UT band. (Tom Raymond)

Mississippi State Coach Jackie Sherrill and I meet at midfield. (TOM RAYMOND)

A nice thought for a Tennessee Christmas, huh? (UNIVERSITY OF TENNESSEE)

CHAPTER • 14

Vanderbilt

For as long as I can remember, we have always closed our regular season against our in-state foe Vanderbilt. The Tennessee-Vanderbilt game for the Vandy players and people is their game of the year. Growing up in the mid-state area and coaching for one year very early in my career at Vanderbilt gave me a unique perspective on what this game means to their program. I told our players just that at the team meeting Sunday night. If they beat us, their season is a success, even if they had lost every other game.

Going into this game, we were pretty banged up. We were coming off of a stretch where we had played several physical games in a row. Al Wilson's shoulder was giving him a great deal of trouble, and we didn't want to play him if we didn't have to. Raynoch Thompson was also hurting, and we hoped to not have to play him. We needed some players to step up for Al and Raynoch, and we needed our whole team to concentrate on the task at hand.

It is sometimes challenging to keep our guys focused on the Vanderbilt game. It was easy to want to look ahead to Atlanta or a bowl game, but this year our guys were focused on the task at hand. We wanted to finish what we had started, and Vanderbilt even helped by tossing some logs on the fire. Several Vandy players were quoted in the newspapers as saying how much they looked forward to ruining our run at the national championship and ruining our unbeaten season.

I probably didn't have to say a whole lot to get our players' attention about this game. The last three times we had played Vandy it had been a

Several Vandy players were quoted in the newspapers as saying how much they looked forward to ruining our run at the national championship.

		DEFENSIVE PRACTICE SCHEDULE		EMPHASIS
	WORKOUT: TUE-KY	DATE: 11-24-98		FAV. RUNS/PA PASS
	GEAR: VOL	TIME: 2:30 MEET 4:05 FLEX		**BOOT / WAGGLE**
	PLACE: U HUDSON	WINNING EDGE: POISE AND PRIDE		
	TACKLES	ENDS	LB'ERS	SECONDARY
1 4:05		TEAM FLEX		
2 4:12		PAT / FG BLOCK		
3 4:15	GET OFF MVMTS	PUNT PUNT	PRO/COVER BLK/RET	
4 4:25	HANDS EXPLOSION (SLED) GET OFF TACKLING	(WINNING SLED WORK SPLIT ZONE	EDGE) W. DRILL M/M TECH	FOOTWORK TACKLING SCREEN DRILL
5 4:32	BLOCK REACT TRAP 3, 4I	COUNTER 1. WRONG ARM 2. HARD JOINT	RUN KEY TRAP CTR. TRAP ZONE	FORMATION ADJ.
6 4:39		TEAM VS. VANDY		
7 4:39		FRONT 7 VS VANDY		1 ON 1 VS. WRs
8 4:56		FRONT 7 VS. VANDY		SEND SAFTIES -------------------- FADE -N- SLANTS
9 5:03		TEAM VS. VANDY		
10 5:13		TEAM VS. VANDY		
11 5:23		PASS RUSH VS. OFF. LINE	O/S	VS. OFFENSE
12 5:30		TEAM VS. VANDY		
13 5:40		TEAM VS. OFFENSE		
14 5:48		CONDITIONING / KICK OFF COV		
15	88			

**Vanderbilt Week Practice Schedules
(text resumes on page 132)**

DEFENSIVE PRACTICE SCHEDULE

EMPHASIS

WORKOUT: THUR-VANDY DATE: 11-26-98 ALL PHASES
GEAR: SHORTS TIME: 8:30 MTG, 10:05 FLEX
PLACE: HUDSON WINNING EDGE: GAME PREPARATION

#	TACKLES	ENDS	LB'ERS	SECONDARY
1 10:05	TEAM	FLEX		
2 4:12	CUB MVMTS DROP HOOK	KICK	OFF COVERAGE	
3	BEAR (EAT BACK) TRAP ZONE	KICK	OFF RETURN	
4	OPP DEAL TRICK	PUNT	PRO/COVER	
5	PUNT	BLOCK	RET	SAFE
6 10:47	TEAM	VS. VANDY		BACKED UP
7 10:57	TEAM	VS. VANDY		OPEN FIELD
8 11:07	TEAM	VS. VANDY		OPEN FIELD
9 11:17	TEAM	VS. VANDY		OPEN FIELD TO ORANGE AREA
10 11:27	TEAM	VS. VANDY		ORANGE AREA TO GOALLINE
11 11:37	TEAM	VS. OFFENSE		2 MINUTE
12 11:47		LAST	TACKLE	
13	88			
14				
15				

dogfight, and most of our juniors and seniors had played in those games. Recently, Vanderbilt had been very good on the defensive side of the football. As I watched the Commodores on film Sunday, it was quite evident they were still more talented on defense than on offense.

I was excited as I watched film on Sunday. Still thrilled with what I thought to be a dominating win over Kentucky, I could see within our grasp a goal that we all had set that is so hard to accomplish—an undefeated regular season in the Southeastern Conference. The mood around our football complex was as upbeat the next few days as I have ever seen it.

After looking at Vanderbilt film for a couple of days and sitting through several offensive and defensive staff meetings, I felt like we had a chance to control the game from the beginning if we didn't continually shoot ourselves in the foot, which we hadn't done much of. Offensively, Vandy had struggled moving the football and scoring many points. Defensively, they were talented, but not quite as skilled as they had been. Vandy, for about three years, had as good a group of linebackers and corners as there were in our league. When they graduated those players, they suffered some drop in talent, but a huge drop in experience. Don't get me wrong, though, Vanderbilt was still a good defensive football team.

Our defensive staff felt like their group could shut Vandy down, as John didn't believe they could run the football much on us. Offensively, we believed one of our signature running plays, the counter trey, would be successful, as would our passing game against Vandy's defense.

Our team practiced well all week. While I mentioned the mood around the football complex, it was also Thanksgiving week. I talked to our players about how much we all had to be thankful for this year. Thursday's practice was especially fun. We have a tradition that in the last home practice our seniors make their "last tackle" on a tackling dummy with a Vanderbilt jersey on it. Our players form two rows and our seniors run right down the middle of them for their "last tackle." It's always a fun day, but that particular practice was as enjoyable a one as I have ever seen. Our football team didn't have a lot of cliques or loners; we had a group that was tight-knit. It really showed this week. We said a special Thanksgiving prayer, and our football team went to join family and friends for the day.

Game day arrived, and our players were ready. They were intent on finishing the season right. As we were running onto the field, we were welcomed with a beautiful site. We were playing in Nashville at Vanderbilt's stadium, but the stands were packed with Big Orange. I can't express how much pride our team felt, and how much pride I felt at that moment in seeing this sea of orange in the stands. It had to be 90 percent filled with Tennessee people. It was an incredible feeling, and it gave our players a tremendous boost of confidence.

While the game was hard-fought, we stayed in control throughout. Our defense controlled the line of scrimmage, and we were able to create turnovers. The defense really stepped up big in shutting Vanderbilt out and actually scored a touchdown on a fumble recovery after a great hit by Eric Westmoreland. Offensively, we scored on a long touchdown pass and moved the football well enough to keep the game out of doubt en route to a 41-0 victory. Perhaps the best thing about this game other than the win, was we got to keep Al and Raynoch out of the game and let them heal.

We were playing in Nashville at Vanderbilt's stadium, but the stands were packed with Big Orange.

In the locker room after the game, I told our team they had just accomplished something that no other Tennessee team had done in their lifetime—finish a regular season 11-0. Not a soul in our locker room was satisfied yet. Even the most casual observer could notice that. We were going to Atlanta the next week to play the Mississippi State Bulldogs in the Southeastern Conference Championship game. We had a title to defend.

We sang our Tennessee Victory Song and climbed another rung on the ladder. Two more to go.

CHAPTER • 15

Mississippi State: The SEC Championship Game

"I can't remember heading into a game as big as this one with as many distractions as our team had." Those were my thoughts and concerns before I looked at the Mississippi State film on Sunday. Our team had just completed a remarkable feat by winning every single regular season game. But our team was faced with distractions, not entirely negative ones, but distractions nonetheless as we headed toward our most important game so far.

The next game was for the Southeastern Conference championship against the Mississippi State Bulldogs. The distractions were something old and something new. The *old* was the B.C.S. In the B.C.S. rankings, we had a lead over UCLA and Kansas State. The rankings were fairly close, and all of the experts predicted it would tighten up substantially if all three of us won. Depending, of course, on which channel you happened to watch or listen, or which newspaper you read, there would be a different prediction of who the top two teams would be, and those would be the two teams that would get to face off in the Fiesta Bowl with the national championship at stake.

The *new* issue concerned my close friend and offensive coordinator, David Cutcliffe. David had been interviewed for the head-coaching job at the University of Mississippi, and the rumors were rampant that he was going to be hired. David was ready to be a head coach. He had been interviewed for head-coaching jobs in our league before, and I knew it

> David wanted a head-coaching job very badly, and he was my friend, so naturally I wanted the best for someone that I loved.

DEFENSIVE PRACTICE SCHEDULE

WORKOUT: TUE-MSU **DATE:** 12-01-98
GEAR: VOL **TIME:** 2:30 MEET   3:55 FLEX
PLACE: U HUDSON **WINNING EDGE:** WIN 1 ON 1 BATTLES

EMPHASIS
FAV. RUNS/PA PASS
BOOT/ WAGGLE

#	TACKLES	ENDS	LB'ERS	SECONDARY
1 4:05		TEAM FLEX		
2 4:12		PAT / FG BLOCK		
3 4:15	GET OFF(CHUTES) MVMTS CHANGE/SLANT	PUNT PUNT	PRO/COVER BLK/RET	
4 4:25	HANDS EXPLOSION GET OFF TACKLE V. BLCKR	(WINNING EDGE) 6 TECH 1. BASE 2. RUB 3. CUT OFF	9 TECH KEY BOOT & WAGGLE	FOOTWORK TACKLING
5 4:32	DBL TEAM BLOCK BACK MVMT TO BLOCKER	MOVEMENT TURNBACK PRO	G SLANT G HARD / DE	FLOW RULE IT "NASTY" BOOT/WAG
6 4:39		TEAM VS. MSU		
7 4:49	VS. CANS/TE FRONT 7	VS. MSU		1 ON 1 VS. WRs
8 4:56	FRONT 7	VS. MSU	←	SAFETIES RELEASES
9 5:04		TEAM VS. MSU →		
10 5:14		TEAM VS. MSU →		
11 5:24	PASS RUSH	VS. OFF. LINE	O/S	VS. OFFENSE
12 5:31		TEAM VS. MSU →		
13 5:41		TEAM VS. OFFENSE →		
14 5:48	KICK OFF COV./	CONDITIONING		
15	88			

Mississippi State Week Practice Schedules
(text resumes on page 138)

DEFENSIVE PRACTICE SCHEDULE

EMPHASIS

WORKOUT: THUR-MSU DATE: 12-03-98 ALL PHASES
GEAR: SHORTS TIME: 2:30 MTG, 4:05 FLEX
PLACE: HUDSON WINNING EDGE: GAME PREPARATION

#	TACKLES	ENDS	LB'ERS	SECONDARY
1 4:05	TEAM	FLEX		
2 4:12	HOOK DROP	KICK	OFF COVERAGE	
3	MVMT. GAMES(HI-LO)	KICK	OFF RETURN	
4	PEEL HARD DRAW TURNBACK PROT.	PUNT	PRO/COVER	
5	PUNT	BLOCK	RET	SAFE
6 4:47	TEAM	VS. MSU		BACKED UP
7 4:57	TEAM	VS. MSU		OPEN FIELD
8 5:07	TEAM	VS. MSU		OPEN FIELD
9 5:17	TEAM	VS. MSU		OPEN FIELD TO ORANGE AREA
10 5:27	TEAM	VS. MSU		ORANGE AREA TO GOALLINE
11 5:37	TEAM	VS. OFFENSE		2 MINUTE
12 5:47	88			
13				
14				
15				

MISSISSIPPI STATE

was just a matter of time before some smart athletic director would hire him. David wanted a head-coaching job very badly, and he was my friend, so naturally I wanted the best for someone I loved.

While I wanted the best for David and highly recommended him to Ole Miss, the timing of things couldn't have been much worse for us. That wasn't anybody's fault, as nobody wants to get behind in recruiting. David had been my offensive coordinator since I got this job, and he was such a steady hand for Tee and our offense. Plus, he was the primary architect for our offensive game plan and our primary play caller.

I know that David viewed the Ole Miss job as a great opportunity. I could only imagine all the things going through his mind as I knew he was down the hall trying his best to concentrate only on our upcoming game against Mississippi State. In a day or two, his future could change dramatically, and that potential change was coming at the point that our team was preparing to play for the right to play in the national-championship game. I decided to talk to our team about these issues, not as distractions but rather as opportunities, and address them as to how we as a team should handle them.

I've mentioned several times about the leadership, character, and maturity of our team. Our players came to Tennessee making choices over other schools to improve themselves. They go to class to get a degree to improve themselves. That is the way life is. If David Cutcliffe could advance professionally, that was what he should do and we were all excited. I intended to take a negative and make it into a positive.

As the team gathered Sunday night, I reminded them of those traits that they had exhibited through our regular season and how they should call on those traits as we tried to finish our climb to the top of the ladder. I talked about the only things we could control and those were how we prepared, practiced, and played. I told our team that opportunities would come to those who showed character, toughness, and perseverance—like the opportunity to play for a championship or to step in for an injured teammate, or the opportunity that David had just earned. I finished by saying when the opportunity presents itself, no matter in what form, a champion will seize it and make the most of it.

Just a short while after talking to our team about opportunities, I introduced David Cutcliffe as the new head coach at Mississippi. I was thrilled for him, although I wished it could have happened after the SEC Championship game. Our team gathered in one of the most emotional moments I remember as a Tennessee player or coach, to hear David tell what these players and our program meant to him. I told our team that the best thing we could do for David was to send him off a winner in his last game as a Tennessee coach. David Cutcliffe had done a lot for our program at Tennessee.

I recognized how vulnerable our team could be with all the goings-on during this championship week. I had watched a lot of Mississippi State film Sunday and Monday and knew they could run the football, and they were daring and physical on defense. State was a very good football team. It was a problem enough just preparing for a team like State, but when you throw in all the B.C.S. controversy and David's imminent departure, my concerns were obvious. As much as I preached about not paying any attention to the B.C.S., the mere thought of winning all of our games and the league championship game and not getting the opportunity to play in the Fiesta Bowl made me sick.

Amazingly, our players' preparation was outstanding. I credit that to not only the leadership and character of our team, but to our staff that had been disciplined all year in dealing with our players. We had preached to them all season about focusing only on the game in front of them or "the next rung on the ladder." I can't recall one player saying a word all week about Kansas State, UCLA, or Florida State.

Mississippi State came into the game in a great position. They were the underdogs, and the media was concentrating on our undefeated season, the B.C.S., and David's getting the Mississippi job. State also had a lot of talented players. Their tailback, James Johnson, was one of the best players in our league. He was a big, bruising tailback, a lot like Jamal. Their offensive line started four seniors. One of their guards, Randy Thomas, was outstanding. They were very good at tight end and had an explosive player, Kevin Prentiss, on the outside and in the return game.

Defensively, they were a nightmare to prepare for. Their defensive alignments were often unique, plus they had a lot of team speed on defense. They had several really athletic guys on defense, with Kevin Sluder and Ed Smith up front being really fine players. Their linebacker, Barrin Simpson, and their corner, Robert Bean, were impressive players. One thing for sure about State defensively is they would bring the heat. If your execution against them was good, you had a chance to make big plays. If your execution was not, it could be a long day at the office.

Those thoughts were exactly what our staff shared with our team all week in practice and meetings. We talked a lot about patience offensively. I knew State would make some plays against us with their defensive calls, but if we were patient we would eventually catch them in vulnerable spots.

I told our team before we left Knoxville that turnovers would determine this game. I reminded them of last year's championship game against Auburn, and I told them we could not afford that against Mississippi State. State's defense fed off turnovers, and their only recipe to win was to force turnovers and be able to run the football. All year long, I said, we had won because we were the most physical team every Saturday when we lined up on the field. Be more physical and protect the football and you'll repeat as champions of your conference. That was how I left it with our team.

Our players were ready to play, and they knew only two rungs were left on the ladder.

Championship day was long. As a coach or player, you would prefer to play early instead of having to wait all day. Because our game was so late, we all watched Miami upset UCLA. While that took some of the suspense out of the B.C.S. rankings, I don't believe that it had any effect on the way that we played Saturday night. Our players were ready to play, and they knew only two rungs were left on the ladder. This next rung was all that mattered right now.

The game was a physical football game. Both defenses played better than their offensive counterparts. I was impressed with the play of State's defense, and they kept the game close until late. We threw an interception early that they returned for a touchdown, and we were not very sharp offensively until late in the game. In the fourth quarter, our guys played like champions. Tee threw a beautiful long pass to Peerless, who made a difficult catch for the go-ahead touchdown. Our defense forced a turnover on State's next possession and immediately Tee threw a strike to Cedrick Wilson for another touchdown to seal the game. It was one of the most beautiful post-corner routes I had ever seen, as we went on to win, 24-14.

When we got our backs to the wall and all the favored teams around us had lost, the character and the will of our team to win took over that night in Atlanta. That's what I told the Southeastern Conference champions in a joyous locker room. Winning the Southeastern Conference Championship is special, and winning it back-to-back makes it more special. We have the toughest league in America. I said all this to my team and told them that the repeat felt sweeter because nobody expected us to. We hugged and laughed and celebrated, and then sang our Tennessee Victory Song. We then sighed a huge sigh of relief, shared a special good-bye with David, and turned our thoughts to Tempe.

After we finished our song, I told our guys that nobody except them really did believe they would be back here celebrating another championship. And nobody really believed we could win the national championship—except the men in this dressing room. Those were the only ones that I cared about on that issue. One more rung climbed; one more rung to go.

CHAPTER • 16

Florida State: The Fiesta Bowl

What an incredible journey our team had been on so far. We had one more place to go—to the desert and Tempe, Arizona, for the national-championship game.

After the Mississippi State game, I ran across so many people who loved Tennessee football. One meeting in particular really struck me: A gentleman stopped me, wished me well, and said, "Coach, I can't really afford to go to Tempe, but my wife and I are going anyway. I want to be a part of history…I want to see the Vols win this national championship."

Talk about turning me inside out. Here is this man, one man who loves the Vols, sacrificing financially to be with the Vols.

I thought, "We've got to win! We've got to win for these loyal people who call themselves Tennessee fans—for all the players that ever put on the orange and white—and for this team of men who had fought so hard.

Boy, it can be lonely at the top!

The Florida State Seminoles were our opponent, a school we had never played as long as I had been associated with Tennessee football.

The morning of the SEC Championship Game, I had anticipated that the next day would be a gut wrencher. I felt like Kansas State, UCLA, and we would all win. I knew that Mississippi State, Texas A&M, and Miami were all quality opponents, but I just believed the three favorites were a little stronger. If that would have happened, one of us would have been left out in the rain and I didn't think it would be us, but you never know. I can tell you when I

DEFENSIVE PRACTICE SCHEDULE — EMPHASIS

WORKOUT: #3 FSU PM DATE: 12-18-98
GEAR: FULL TIME: 3:00 MTG, 3:45 FLEX
PLACE: STADIUM WINNING EDGE: TEAM SWARM

# / Time	TACKLES	ENDS	LB'ERS	SECONDARY
1 — 3:45	TEAM FLEX			
2 — 3:52		KICK	OFF COVERAGE	
3 — 3:59	O/S TECH I/S TECH	(WINNING EDGE) TACKLE MOVEMENT VS. SCHEME	W DRILL MEDICINE BALL ANGLE TACKLE	FOOTWORK & BALL DRILLS
4 — 4:09	PASS RUSH TACKLE QB	MAX X VS. FAN PRO SCREEN CUT	SPOT DRILL ------------- PASS DROPS	RELEASES SQUAT TECH
5 — 4:19	FRONT 7	VS. FSU		1 ON 1 VS. WRs
6 — 4:29	PASS RUSH	VS. OFF LINE	O/S VS.	OFFENSE
7 — 4:39	TEAM	VS. FSU		
8 — 4:49	TEAM	VS. FSU		
9 — 4:59	TEAM	VS. OFFENSE		
10 — 5:09	YOUNG	CONDITIONING PLAYERS	INDIVIDUAL	
11 — 5:19	TEAM	VS. OFFENSE	YOUNG PLAYERS	
12 — 5:29	88			
13				
14				
15				

Florida State Week Practice Schedules
(text resumes on page 147)

Kicker Jeff Hall gets the ball into the air at the Fiesta Bowl. (TOM RAYMOND)

Defensive back Steve Johnson awaits Florida State nemesis Peter Warrick. (TOM RAYMOND)

The idea was to put the clamps on Florida State when they tried to spread us out. (TOM RAYMOND)

Travis Stephens turns upfield against Florida State. (TOM RAYMOND)

Peerless Price catches the ball and sets sail for a spectacular touchdown play in the Fiesta Bowl.
(TOM RAYMOND)

Everyone who's for Tennessee, stand up and cheer! (Tom Raymond)

Defensive tackle Billy Ratliff makes a beeline for the Florida State quarterback. (Tom Raymond)

The scoreboard tells the story.
(UNIVERSITY OF TENNESSEE)

I respect Florida State coach Bobby Bowden, and I hope to see him again this year…at the Sugar Bowl.
(TOM RAYMOND)

What a nice sight!
(UNIVERSITY OF TENNESSEE)

I really don't remember what I said, but I sure felt good. (UNIVERSITY OF TENNESSEE)

Victory is sweet, but now it's time to point to '99. (UNIVERSITY OF TENNESSEE)

DEFENSIVE PRACTICE SCHEDULE — EMPHASIS

WORKOUT: #4 FSU
GEAR: VOL
PLACE: Hudson
DATE: 12-19-98
TIME: 8:30 Meet 9:45 Flex
WINNING EDGE: Respect

# / Time	TACKLES	ENDS	LB'ERS	SECONDARY
1 9:45		Team Flex		
2 :52		PAT/FG Block		
3 :55	Get off Movement Fit (Hat)	Get off movement Shuttle	W Dr.11 / Spot Dr.11 / Take-on	FOOTWORK / HANDS DRILLS
4 10:05	Tackling Sled (Dbl)(3,4,5 Combo)	5 Tech SlimTech / 9 Tech Drops Rak	Pass Drop / S/F Tech	SQUAT TECH 1/2 Field
5 :15	Front 7 vs FSU			1 on 1 vs WR's
6 :25	Pass Rush Tech	Pass Rush Tech PA	O/S vs Off.	
7 :35	Team vs FSU			
8 :45	Team vs FSU			
9 :55	Team vs Offense			
10 11:05	Young Players Ind.			
11 :15	Team vs Offense (young players)			
12	88			
13				
14				

FLORIDA STATE 145

DEFENSIVE PRACTICE SCHEDULE   EMPHASIS

WORKOUT: #5 (FSU)   DATE: 12-19-98
GEAR: Full   TIME: 3:00 Meet 4:00 Flex
PLACE: N/T complex   WINNING EDGE: Respect

#	Time	TACKLES	ENDS	LB'ERS	SECONDARY
1	4:00	Team Flex			
2	4:07	GotoFF Hands/Eyes G.L. Drills	Get off Sled Work	Take on Drill / mim Tech	FOOTWORK RELEASES
3	:17	Pass Rush 3 man Max - Rock -		KEY DRILL	
4	:27	Front 7 vs FSU			1 on 1 vs WR's
5	:37	Team vs FSU			
6	:47	Team vs FSU			
7	:57	Team vs Offense			
8	5:07	Team vs Offense			Blitz
9	:17	88			
10					
11					
12					
13					
14					

woke up Sunday morning in Atlanta I was so relieved—not only that we beat Mississippi State, but that we didn't have to depend on polls, computers, etc.

The next week was busy for me travelwise and phone-call-wise. On Monday morning, I left to go to the National Football Foundation College Hall of Fame awards in New York City. This is a great college football event and almost every head coach in the country is there. Tennessee has had a remarkable number of inductees. I especially wanted to go to see Doug Dickey be honored by the Foundation as the Athletic Director of the Year.

Vicky and I had a great time in New York, even though the number of phone calls and requests for interviews were increasing by the minute. I saw a lot of my coaching friends in the two days there and received a lot of congratulations, encouragement, and even a few tips. All the tips were appreciated and some of them were even used. I'll be honest, the words I heard the most were, "Coach, congratulations and good luck. Florida State sure is great defensively." All the tips about their defense were right.

Speaking of well-wishers, Steve Spurrier dropped by the table I was sitting at the night of the induction and told me good luck and that he was pulling for us. I know a lot of Tennessee fans won't believe that, but I've got witnesses. He said it loud enough that Vicky and others heard it. Steve was gracious and I appreciated him coming by to visit.

I got back from New York Wednesday night and went straight to the office from the airport to get my first look at Florida State on film. Our staff had looked at them the day before, but I was anxious to see them. Believe me, they were everything people had been telling me about them—especially on defense. They were just outstanding.

Wednesday night, I got back to making recruiting calls until late. I had worked the phones in New York and always attempted to make recruiting calls a priority. I was able to make telephone calls until late to the West Coast because of the time difference. After making my calls I spent some time working on the practice schedule, both in Knoxville and Tempe. Our players were in final exams now.

> Steve Spurrier dropped by the table I was sitting at...and told me good luck and that he was pulling for us.

FLORIDA STATE   147

Thursday, Vicky and I left to go to Orlando, Florida, where I received the Eddie Robinson National Coach of the Year award at the ESPN College Football Banquet. I was humbled by this award because I believe that they really should give awards to teams and assistant coaches. Football is a team effort. I couldn't help but think as I was walking up to the podium to receive this award on national television just how blessed I've been. Growing up in Winchester, Tennessee, I thought how many people from Franklin County and other places I've lived had helped me to be in this position. It was just an overwhelming feeling. Al Wilson was also there, and he was named to the All-America team.

I remember feeling on top of the world at these awards until somebody from ABC or ESPN asked me how good I thought Florida State was. My thoughts immediately were recentered to what was really important. The game was left. Every honor, award, and gesture is special, but the most special thing remained in front of us. My mind abruptly left the goings-on of the awards and banquets and shifted back to the game mode.

The next day I had to fly to Arizona for a joint press conference with Coach Bobby Bowden for the Fiesta Bowl. We flew there and straight back. Florida State and the national championship game were twenty-five days away.

By the weekend, our staff had broken down all of the Florida State film. Some guys were on the road recruiting, and I was about to hit the road every night for the next ten or twelve days. But both John Chavis and Randy Sanders were in town, and I had my first chance to visit at length about FSU on tape with the guys responsible for making the calls against the Seminoles.

After watching them myself and talking to John and Randy, who both had watched them a lot by now, one thing was abundantly clear—they were fast. They reminded me a lot of us in many ways. Tremendous team speed and a whole lot of guys who looked and played like one another on defense, and a couple of terribly dangerous guys on offense were the trademarks of this team. Offensively, they had three guys who could take it to the house on you in a second. Their wideout, Peter Warrick, is one of the premier players in college football. You couldn't miss him on tape: He was the guy who scored a touchdown seemingly every time he had the ball.

Warrick was a threat not only as a receiver but also on reverses in which he ran or passed the ball, and in the return game. I knew about him because we had tried to recruit him three years earlier when he was a standout high school quarterback. You could tell he was going to be a special player. It was clear to me that we had to limit Peter Warrick's opportunities in the passing game to have a chance to win.

Their tailback, Travis Minor, clearly appeared to be a game breaker. Minor was a scatback, a guy who had great balance and speed and quickness. He was not going to run over a lot of guys, but if you didn't lay a lick on him he could really make you pay. Minor reminded me a lot of John Avery, the Ole Miss player of the last couple of years, because both guys weren't big, but they were electrifying. Travis Minor didn't mind taking it up inside, but he was most effective if he got outside with the football.

Their other wide receiver, Laveranues Coles, was another really fast player. He could really stretch your defense and you couldn't pay too much attention to Warrick or Coles could beat you, too.

Their offensive line was really big and good looking, but it was not the most-experienced area of their team. They were somewhat like us there; they had a few injuries and a lot of their best days were ahead of them. Florida State had its starting quarterback injured late in the year and turned to a young sophomore, Marcus Outzen, who had performed exceptionally well in their victory over Florida. Outzen had not played a lot until the end of the year, but you could tell he was a really good athlete. When he saw or felt a little pressure, Outzen would tuck it in and run. Unlike a lot of quarterbacks who tuck and run when they feel any pressure, this guy could run. In fact, he was probably a more dangerous runner than passer. Outzen had thrown the ball well enough, however, to keep Florida honest. So, we knew this guy was plenty good enough to make big plays in a huge game and lead his team to victory. Marcus Outzen was not the kind of football player that could win the game or turn it all by himself, but with the proper help could hold up his end of the bargain with a winning effort.

Defensively, they were special. They played with four ends, and I couldn't tell which group was better. Their starters, Roland Seymour and Tony Bryant, and the second group, Jamal Reynolds and David Warren, were all outstanding players. All four of these guys could hold their ground in the running game, and all could really come off the corners when you threw the ball.

Their tackles were really good as well. They rotated four or five guys, like we try to do, at the position and all of them could play. Number 53, Corey Simon, popped out at you on film. He was a dominating, disruptive kind of inside player that every program looks for when recruiting.

This front group had held their opponents to an unbelievable number of net-loss running plays. All their front guys had quickness, which allows penetration. I knew it would be vital for our offensive line to come off the ball hard every play.

Their linebackers were fast and active. Florida State's defensive philosophy is to bunch up and shoot the gaps and bring lots of pressure. Their linebackers were more important to them in stopping the run than they were in pass defense.

Their defense called for linebackers to be run stoppers and to create difficult down-and-distance situations for their opponents. Their linebackers were very aggressive and good at this. If the Florida State defense was successful, and they often were, offensive teams would face obvious passing situations. FSU would then substitute wholesale, getting their best pass rushers and extra coverage men in and take some of their linebackers out.

Their pressure package is clearly effective because they had secondary guys who could cover and make plays. They had some long, tall guys back there who could obviously run. I was particularly impressed with one of their corners, Mario Edwards, who made a bunch of interceptions. They led the nation in defense. Suffice it to say, they were really good.

When you play pressure as I've said before, you get a lot of one-on-one match-ups. In looking at Florida State throughout the year, their corners were matched up a lot one on one. What happened mostly, though, was the opposing quarterback had so much pressure he either couldn't throw, or he had to throw too early. One thing about FSU and their pressure, if you wanted to beat them deep you must really execute with a good pattern, throw and reception—most of all protection of the quarterback. The reason is simple: With their speed in the secondary and the speed and pressure from their front people, you are left with little room for error.

> **Florida State's defensive philosophy is to bunch up and shoot the gaps and bring lots of pressure.**

As we planned, our offensive staff did see something that really caught our attention in the FSU-North Carolina State game. N.C. State was able to throw over the top on FSU on play-action a couple of times. They froze the secondary just a little with play-action and N.C. State's great receiver, Torry Holt, got behind the secondary and made the play. To beat FSU deep, you had better have a guy outside who could make a play. Fortunately, we just happened to have one.

As far as special teams go, it didn't take long to see they were special there, too. Their kicker had a cannon for a leg and was an accurate guy. Their punting game was solid. Their return game, because of their speed, was outstanding. They had used Warrick some in the return game, and I told our staff to expect to see him back there.

The next week we started practice in Knoxville. I decided to leave the day after Christmas to go to Tempe. That would give us a little over a week to begin our preparations and practice for FSU. Our team was excited, as you might imagine, with the game of their lives coming up and the holiday season upon us. It's easy to forget, with so much at stake, that the battle you're going to fight will be decided by young men, usually eighteen to twenty-one years old. Even with the excitement of Christmas, the trip, and the game, our team was mentally focused throughout the pre-Christmas practices. To be honest with you, our team had a little bit of an edge to it.

After the regular season, we were ranked number one in both polls. But the experts declared us to be the underdogs to Florida State. That didn't sit well with our guys, especially a few of the seniors. In those first few days and practices after the regular season, I heard a whole lot of talking from our players about "not getting enough respect." The leaders on our football team seized this underdog role and ran with it. They were genuinely upset about it. I didn't try to discourage their feelings, fact is, when opportunities presented themselves I poured a little gas on the fire.

We kept our practices in Knoxville short and crisp. Our film-study time at this point was crucial and the scouting report on FSU was completed before we left for Tempe. Our plan was in, we were healthy, and our attitude was exceptional as we looked forward to playing for it all. Our last practice was on Wednesday, December 23, and I told our guys that respect wasn't handed out, it was earned. I told them that come January 4, they would have an opportunity to earn the respect of the nation and to be the consensus national champions. I warned them that they first had to manage themselves well off the field during the holidays and in Tempe. Then we had to practice like champions when we got to the desert if they were really serious about earning respect.

Actually, our team had already earned tremendous respect from their accomplishments thus far. They certainly had earned *my* utmost respect. I have to admit I liked the way our team was looking at this game when we broke for Christmas. I really felt good about our chances, even though I knew Florida State was outstanding.

Being home the entire Christmas Day was just a wonderful present for our staff and their families. Every year, it seemed, we've left for our bowl game on Christmas Day because of January 1 bowl dates. That meant packing and planning sometimes had to take priority over being able to relax and celebrate the holiday season with your family. I know I earned lots of brownie points for being home all day Christmas, and I'll bet every person on our staff did. I had a wonderful family Christmas. Now, I did spend a little time Christmas Eve and Christmas Day in preparation for the Fiesta Bowl, and I squeezed in a few recruiting calls, but mostly I enjoyed Christmas.

Most of our players went to their homes at Christmas and were allowed to fly to Arizona from their hometown if they wished. For our out-of-state players, this allowed them to spend a lot more time with their families. Every one arrived in Tempe on the evening of the 26th.

A bowl trip is supposed to be a reward for a good season. It sometimes can become a tough call for a coach on where to draw the line on fun and work. We've been to a bowl game every year since I've been the head coach at Tennessee, and my philosophy has been pretty simple. Our priority is in preparing and practicing for the game. What opportunities for fun we have come after the work is done. There are always plenty of those.

I've also learned some great lessons about planning bowl itineraries. We do our work, meetings, and mental preparation, and the bowl people work around us, not visa versa. If you're not careful, the bowl people will dominate your schedule and disrupt your preparations.

This bowl trip was different. Not only was it for the national championship, but it was the inaugural championship game in the now famous Bowl Championship Series. The number of media in Tempe to cover our game was staggering. I knew there would be a lot, but the number was even greater than I had anticipated.

I talked to our entire team about the media crunch that they were about to face in Knoxville before we broke for Christmas, and I brought it up again in Tempe at our first team meeting there. I wasn't worried so much about our players' saying something that wasn't becoming to our program or something that would incite our opponent. I was worried about them getting distracted from the constant questions and losing focus in our practices and team meetings that followed all the scheduled and unscheduled interviews. I talked to our Unity Council members and senior captains about this and asked them to help me guard against this. I also made it clear to Bud Ford and Haywood Harris that there was time allotted for this, and we would not change.

Our team was headquartered at the Scottsdale Plaza, and there were an unbelievable number of Tennessee fans that came by the hotel to get autographs, pictures, or just to see our players. The University of Tennessee has the best traveling fans in the nation. Actually, we have the best and most loyal fans, period. I was somewhat concerned by the tremendous attention paid to our team by fans, as again I didn't want them to be distracted by things they normally don't see so much of in the course of the season. I took comfort when I thought about our captains and our Unity Council, as I could count on them to help provide focus and encouragement. We also had a great plan regarding security people to help the players to and from events. Experience is a great teacher.

By the time we got to Tempe, we really had our game plan in place. Our scout team had been trying to simulate FSU the last few days of practice in Knoxville. After a day of getting our travel legs back under us, we immediately picked right up where we left off in Knoxville. Our practices every day were sharp and crisp. I know you hear most coaches say they practice great every day, but I'm really pretty honest about that when we don't.

In Tempe, we had excellent practices every single day. A good practice is when you are fundamentally sound in your technique, focused on your responsibilities, and effort and enthusiasm is at a high level. I credit that to the maturity, character, and leadership of our team. My emphasis was our fundamentals. I worked the practice schedules to get what I wanted. Sometimes you can get caught up in scheming and forget about what got you here: blocking and tackling and taking care of the football. I had to intervene a couple of times, but the point was well made with our coaches and players.

We wanted to keep firing off the ball and make them a little impatient defensively.

Our staff, team, and individual meetings went well. Guys were alert and attentive. I didn't feel in the days leading up to the game that the massive attention from media and fans was bothering our team. I still kind of got the feeling they were still on that "respect" mission. Respect, however, is not just something you earn or don't earn on the football field. For example, I had to send one young man home the first day. He had been disrespectful to an employee of the hotel. I made it clear to the team that we are here for business, and proper behavior was part of that business.

The players and coaches on our team knew what we must do to beat Florida State. The formula for winning was no different than the one we had when we opened the season more than four months earlier. We had to be more physical than the Seminoles. We had to be able to run the ball, and we had to stop the run.

Offensively, I believed it paramount that our offensive line control the line of scrimmage. I knew we would have running plays where they simply had the numbers on us and would hold us to minimal gains, but even on those plays we had to be physical and take the fight to them. Doing that, I felt, would pay off in the second half. Further, I believed that we needed to be patient and stay with the running game even when they were bunched up on us. Play calling has to be very disciplined here because the easy thing to do is call a pass every time it's second down and you have eight, nine, or ten yards to go. That plays into FSU's hand. We wanted to keep firing off the ball and make them a little impatient defensively. I believed our rushing game had enough strength and discipline to push them off the ball some and gain positive yards without turning it over. We had to penetrate their strength and that was their defensive front.

Our plan was to keep running and hopefully get their corners and safeties up and try to hit it big over the top. We all thought we could suck them in on play-action and get Peerless deep, just as N.C. State had done earlier in the year with Torry Holt. Randy and our offensive guys felt if we got tight man coverage out there we ought to go for the score on the deep outs, corner routes, or the post. We practiced and practiced this in Tempe. Tee was throwing the ball great and his timing with Peerless and our other receivers was excellent.

Defensively, we had to decide whether we were going to play FSU the same way we'd played everybody else, or whether to change some because of the presence of their great player, Warrick. We decided to dance with the one that brought us. Our plan called for our best corner, Dwayne Goodrich, to play Warrick the whole game. We then would match Steve Johnson, our other fine corner cover, on Coles and play both receivers straight up. We were going to come after Outzen with all we had and make him beat us.

All of these defensive plans were predicated on our being able to shut down their running game. Our defensive staff believed we could control the line of scrimmage and make it difficult for them to run. We didn't think Florida State would test us much in the middle, but we thought they would try to run Travis Minor outside and use the draw some to give him some space in which to work. This meant that our linebackers would have lots of open-field-tackle opportunities. They needed to play well, and I was confident they would. Linebacker had really been a strength for us all year.

The eight days I had in Arizona before the game were all about the same. We had meetings in the morning at 7:00 A.M., followed by practice, media obligations, staff meetings, and some work late in the evenings in my room. I had a couple of official Fiesta Bowl activities, including the Fiesta Bowl Ball that I attended. But other than that, it was work—fun work, exciting work—but work nonetheless.

I stayed so busy that I probably didn't reflect enough on the historical meaning of the moment. I was coaching in a game of real historical significance, not only for my university that was hoping for its first national championship in football in forty-seven years but also for college football, which was playing its first true championship football game. I guess I was just too busy worrying about figuring out how to win the game and preparing for it to appreciate the meaningfulness of the moment.

I also really didn't spend much time thinking about how long it had been since Tennessee had won the championship, or how much attention we were getting, or how many people would watch us on ABC. I did spend a lot of time worrying about winning the game for our team because they had fought so hard and worked so hard, and I worried that a loss in the game would be such a bitter pill to a team that already had accomplished so much.

There are two moments I want to share with you when it came to my addressing our team before the Fiesta Bowl. The first was the day before the game at our team meeting, which usually involves a pretty detailed and lengthy meeting with my talking to our team about all the player assignments and the like. It had been reported, or one of our players had heard, that lots of teams and coaches are intimidated when they play against Florida State and Bobby Bowden. I heard a couple of our players say something about that the evening before.

I went into that team meeting and told our players that I wasn't the least bit intimidated by Bobby Bowden.

I went into that team meeting and told our players that I wasn't the least bit intimidated by Bobby Bowden. I said that I respected him, but I wasn't intimidated and resented anyone saying that. I said all of that in about a minute or less and I can tell you every single player in that room was eyeball to eyeball with me. I walked out of that meeting room to complete silence. My staff told me later that really stoked the fire into our players.

The other moment was in the hotel before we left to go to the stadium. Believe me, it was impossible to not be tense at this moment. We'd all been waiting for this very evening all of our lives. The tension was so thick you could cut it with a knife. I started out by telling our guys that the world was getting ready to watch them, that most of the entire nation would be watching on television, even the president of the United States. I told them that Vice President Al Gore was here, along with senators, governors, movie stars, and pro athletes. I continued on and said, "But do you know who called me to wish us well and is glued to the television right now back in Knoxville?" As soon as I said this, every head bobbed up and their eyes got wide with wonder. "Ace Clement called, and all the Lady Vols are glued in right about now." At first they didn't know what to do, they looked at each other, then smiled, then laughed. One of our players had dated Ace for a while, and all of our guys were crazy about her and the Lady Vols. The tension was all gone.

I went through our reminders, told them what a great opportunity that they had, how much I admired them for all they had accomplished, and how much I looked forward to this game.

The locker room was great: excitement, intensity, electricity…we were ready. The players dressed, and John Stucky and the strength staff worked with those who needed extra stretching. Mike Rollo and his staff got all the taping done, and Roger Frazier and Max Parrott put final touches on equipment. They looked like gladiators ready for battle: They *were* gladiators that had fought to the final battle.

The conditions for the game were ideal. The scene was beautiful. I felt confident. I believed we had prepared well enough to win and were good enough to win. Our players were confident—anxious, but confident.

As I always do in pre-game warm-ups, I watched the kicking, then the quarterbacks and wide receivers throwing and catching, then the secondary and linebackers, and, finally, the offensive and defensive lines. It's a routine I enjoy.

I almost always see the head coach for a few minutes at midfield. Coach Bowden and I had had several official functions and duties together during the week, so we had exchanged our normal compliments already. He is a fine man and a fine coach and I enjoyed him. At midfield we talked about our teams and a few of the players we had both wanted, especially Jared Jones, who was their backup quarterback whom I thought we might see some of, especially if we got to Outzen like I hoped we would. Coach Bowden seemed very relaxed, and, surprisingly, I was, too. We shook hands and he said something to the effect that he was just an old coach and that as a young coach, I should cooperate and let them win. It was all in jest and good nature, but I assured him I couldn't help him.

I noticed the orange sunset glowing over the desert mountains. I liked that as I rejoined the pre-game warm-ups.

We went through our reminders one more time. As we went through our tradition of the game maxims, I thought about every Tennessee coach, starting with General Neyland, and how they had gone through the maxims, too, but never prior to a unified national-championship game. As we recited the maxims, the players' voices rang deep and confident, their eyes glued to the list of maxims that had drawn us to this moment in history. That moment will forever be special to these young warriors and all who were present. We were ready.

As we prayed the Lord's Prayer, their voices were bold. As we moved to the door you could feel the anticipation. It was an unbelievable feeling.

Something important happened before we took the field. A gentleman tried to stop me at the door and told me we had to wait for FSU to go to the tunnel first. That made no sense to me. They were going to go past our locker room, make us wait, and probably taunt us as they went by. This was my first decision of the night and the game hadn't even started. No, we were going to the tunnel first, and the Seminoles would have to wait for us. He didn't like it, but we went. Our team loved it as I told the guy to move or he might get run over. We went first, FSU waited for us. To me, logistically, it made all the sense in the world, and strategically we had struck the first blow.

I led our team through the tunnel onto the Fiesta Bowl field for the kick-off. I can't tell you everything that was going through my mind, but I do remember seeing all that orange in the crowd. It made me think of Tennessee people, so many who had longed for so long for this moment. I wanted so badly to win for our team, and for them.

Florida State got outside on us early in the first quarter and made some big yardage, which concerned me. We adjusted some and shut down their running game pretty well. Our offensive line was neutralizing their defensive front and taking the fight to Florida State. We scored first on a well-executed pass play from the four-yard line, a good call, from Tee to Shawn Bryson. We had kicked a field goal a moment earlier, but a Florida State penalty had given us a first down inside the five-yard line, so we opted to not take the field goal and instead go for the touchdown. This was a tough series for me, because taking three points off the scoreboard is a tough call. Most people would say not to do that, but I thought we had a very good goal-line passing plan. The results of this call turned out well for us.

Within minutes, Dwayne Goodrich stepped in front of Peter Warrick and picked off a pass and took it back for a touchdown. That play happened right in front of me and I can't tell you how thrilling it was. I felt at that moment that this was our night.

Later in the game, just as we had planned, Tee hit Peerless off a play-action for a long touchdown. We converted a fourth-and-one late, with another pass and catch from Tee to Bryson.

Our defense kept FSU in check for most of the game, with Goodrich and Johnson holding Warrick to one catch. I thought the most physical team won the game. Our offensive front and defensive front neutralized or won the majority of the battles—remember, games are won at the line of scrimmage.

There was less than a minute to go and we had the ball and the lead and they couldn't stop the clock. It started to sink in. We were just about to win the national championship. I thought of the utter happiness and fulfillment that our players, coaches, and Tennessee fans were about to experience. Coaches and players were hugging. The full-scale celebration was about to begin.

As the last few seconds ticked away on our 23-16 victory, I felt the push from the sideline and I began to jog toward midfield. Lots of people were already starting to run onto the field. I heard lots of shouting and screaming and saw the most people with cameras that I had ever seen in my life. Camera flashes were going like crazy. My mind flashed back to a scene about a year ago for a split second until someone shouted "Coach Fulmer, look at me!" I looked, and saw not a person, but an army of photographers. They had their cameras aimed at me and the orange of the Tennessee Volunteers. That was a perfect moment to end a perfect season. We had climbed to the top of the ladder and we were at the top—the Tennessee Volunteers were national champions.

Coach Bowden was very gracious as we shook hands. It felt like mountains of people were pulling and pushing at us. I had gotten my wife and children to the sidelines as planned—their being at my side was important to me, because they pay such a dear price to be a coach's wife or child. We were all pulled together and the last thing Coach Bowden said was, "I'll see you in New Orleans." I said, "I'll be there." We both have young teams and, who knows, we might just meet again.

As we were led to the stage and podium to address our fans and the nation and to receive the Sears Trophy, I couldn't help but think of my dad who died in 1989: He would have loved to have seen this. The scene on the podium was incredible. Having accomplished the ultimate for our program and being able to share the moment with Vicky, Phillip Jr. and his wife Donna, Courtney, Brittany, and Allison…seeing the incredible smile on Tee Martin and Dwayne Goodrich and Peerless Price and looking into the thousands of Tennessee fans as they cheered—all that was an awesome mountaintop experience.

I couldn't tell you one thing I said. I only hope it was appropriate. But I knew one thing for sure as I stood there and thought of all the Tennessee faithful—I knew I loved this football team and I love Tennessee football.